Phil Maggitti

Bulldogs

Everything about Purchase, Care,
Nutrition, Breeding, Behavior, and Training

With 49 Color Photographs

Illustrations by Tana Hakanson Monsalve

BARRON'S

About the Author

Phil Maggitti is a freelance writer and editor living in a land of virtual reality. His forwarding address is: http://home.ptd.net/~heyphil/phil.html.

Other Barron's titles by Phil Maggitti:
Birman Cats: *A Complete Pet Owner's Manual* (1996)
Before You Buy That Kitten (1995)
Pugs: A Complete Pet Owner's Manual (1994)
Guide to a Well-behaved Cat (1993)
Scottish Fold Cats: A Complete Pet Owner's Manual (1993)

Photo Credits

Joan Balzarini: pages 37, 57 (bottom left), 60 (top).
Zig Leszczynski: pages 12 and 56.
Bonnie Nance: pages 4, 8, 13, 57 (top), 61 (top), and 92.
Judith Strom: pages 21, 41 (bottom), 45, 57, (bottom right), 60 (bottom), 64 (bottom), 68 (both), and 72.
Jean Wentworth: pages 32 (bottom), 53, and 64 (top).
Paulette Braun: All other photos.

Cover Photos

Zig Leszczynski: front cover and inside back cover
Judith Strom: inside front cover
Bonnie Nance: back cover

All inquiries should be addressed to:
Barron's Educational Series, Inc.
250 Wireless Boulevard
Hauppauge, NY 11788

International Standard Book No. 0-8120-9309-7

Library of Congress Catalog Card No. 97-20248

Library of Congress Cataloging-in-Publication Data
Maggitti, Phil.
    Bulldogs : everything about purchase, care, nutrition, breeding, behavior, and training / Phil Maggitti ; illustrations by Tana Hakanson.
        p.   cm. — (A complete pet owner's manual)
    Includes bibliographical references (p. 90) and index.
    ISBN 0-8120-9309-7
    1. Bulldog. I. Title. II. Series.
SF429.B85M24   1997
636.72—dc21   97-20248
                                                CIP

Printed in Hong Kong

987654321

Important Notes

This pet owner's guide tells the reader how to buy and care for a bulldog. The author and the publisher consider it important to point out that the advice given in the book is meant primarily for normally developed puppies from a good breeder—that is, dogs of excellent physical health and good character.

Anyone who adopts a fully grown dog should be aware that the animal has already formed its basic impressions of human beings. The new owner should watch the animal carefully, including its behavior toward humans, and should meet the previous owner. If the dog comes from a shelter, it may be possible to get some information on the dog's background and peculiarities there. There are dogs that, as a result of bad experiences with humans, behave in an unnatural manner or may even bite. Only people that have experience with dogs should take in such animals.

Caution is further advised in the association of children with dogs, in meeting with other dogs, and in exercising the dog without a leash.

Even well-behaved and carefully supervised dogs sometimes do damage to someone else's property or cause accidents. It is therefore in the owner's interest to be adequately insured against such eventualities, and we strongly urge all dog owners to purchase a liability policy that covers their dog.

Contents

Bronco Muggins, all-pro strong safety for the United States Bulldogs.

Preface

Authors generally choose one of three options in writing the preface for a book: They tell the readers in tedious, chapter-by-chapter detail all the wise and wonderful things contained in the pages that will follow. Or, authors present what they consider is a particularly interesting bit of information for which they could not find space in the book. Finally, some desperate writers engage in stream-of-unconsciousness random advertisements for themselves and/or their present states of mind.

The first option is trite and unnecessary, especially if the book has a table of contents and the reader has the wits to consult it. The last choice is self-indulgent. Besides, the states of most writers' minds often border the state of confusion. Therefore, I will choose the second option and will offer, much as a dog hopefully offers a freshly chewed article of his owner's clothing, an interesting reflection on the status of the bulldog in American society.

When last anyone counted, at least 38 institutions of higher learning—and countless institutions of lower and elementary learning as well—were known as "The Bulldogs." Many of those schools are represented by living, breathing, snuffling bulldog mascots. Perhaps the most famous is Uga (pronounced UH-gah), the mascot of the University of Georgia.

Uga V, the latest in a series of Ugas, made news in November 1996 when he tried to bite an Auburn wide receiver who had just caught a 21-yard pass in the Georgia end zone. As fortune would have it, the incident was recorded by a photographer covering the game. Not surprisingly, many Georgia fans wanted a copy. "Seeing him try to take a bite of an Auburn player really warmed my heart," said a Montgomery, Alabama lawyer who ordered a copy of the photo for Christmas.

The lawyer was one of 200 people who wanted to own that Kodak moment. Others included former Georgia coach Vince Dooley and Georgia football trainers, who planned to hang a blowup in the training room. The image was named the Associated Press of Alabama's "Photo of the Month" for November, and, in case you did not hear, Georgia won the game, 56–49, in four overtimes.

Prefaces are also the places in which authors wax humble and then proceed to thank everyone and his or her grandmother for valuable assistance rendered in the production of the book at hand. My humble pie is a small one.

My friend Charlotte Creeley, a self-described "dog trainer, writer, and occasional lawyer from Brockton, Massachusetts," reviewed the chapter on obedience for me. I trust I was able to remove all the mistakes she pointed out.

Otherwise, there is no one else to thank for this production except the countless bands, Rusted Root and others too numerous to mention, whose CDs kept me from falling asleep as the original deadline for this manuscript receded in the rearview mirror of the night like a one-horse town in the middle of a darkened prairie.

Phil Maggitti
Summer 1997

First Considerations

The reason for acquiring a bulldog is far more important than the means by which a bulldog is acquired. A dog is not a fashion statement, a political assertion, or a declaration of moral superiority. Thus, acquiring a bulldog is a personal decision for which you need not have to answer to anyone but yourself and those with whom you live. If you make that decision for the wrong reason, however, you will not be the only one to suffer the consequences. So make the decision wisely.

Why Do You Want a Bulldog?

Companionship

We all know that dogs are good for us. They are always ready to assist at nap time, mealtime, bedtime, and all the other times of our lives. They are matchless at keeping secrets, at keeping us amused, and at keeping loneliness at bay. They have even been credited with lowering our blood pressure, increasing our life spans, and enriching our vocabularies—witness expressions such as dog tired, dog days, hair of the dog, and so on.

Given a dog's innumerable talents, the best reason for getting any dog, especially a bulldog, is to enjoy the pleasure of its company. If you have never experienced the joy of watching a puppy come to terms with the world—and trying to bend the world to its terms—your life is poorer for want of that experience. Puppies are all eyes, flapping ears, and panting innocence. They are fetchingly soft, unerringly cute, endearingly klutzy, and unfailingly energetic. They can make

you laugh when you do not have an inclination or a reason to, and they can coax a smile from your soul on the most grim, cheerless days.

In order to deserve companionship, however, you must be willing to provide it. If you do not enrich your puppy's life as much as she enriches yours, you are taking advantage of her good nature. Your puppy will always be ready to lick your face when the heel marks of a frustrating day are stamped across your brow. When you are keyed up because of something the boss, the clerk at the convenience store, the person in the next cubicle at work, the president, some editorial writer, a loved one, the neighbor's kid, or some fool on the Internet did or said recently, your puppy will be happy to sit and listen to you complain about the unfairness of it all. If you are a good puppy owner, you will be ready to return the favor.

A Playmate for the Kids

"We are given children to test us and to make us more spiritual," wrote columnist George F. Will. Unfortunately, some parents give their children pets for similar reasons; but pets are not teaching devices, and spirituality is beyond the reach of most adults, let alone children. Parents, therefore, should never buy a pet for their children "only if you promise that you're going to take care of it. Or else I'll take it back." Children will make that promise faster than most politicians will accept a plea bargain, but if the child reneges on that promise, Mom or Dad winds up taking care of the pet, and the child has learned the rewards of irresponsibility. Or if, heaven forbid, the parent makes good on the threat to get rid of the pet, the child learns that pets are disposable commodities, a lesson that is brought home all too often in this society.

Bulldogs can inspire a sense of responsibility in children, but children should never be forced to take care of dogs. Parents must also remember that when they buy puppies for their youngsters, they are buying those puppies for themselves. Inevitably, even the most dog-responsible youngsters grow up and leave home; and they do not always take their dogs with them, especially when they go off to college.

Taking care of the family pet provides many people with their first taste of what it is like to be responsible for another living being. This responsibility can do wonders for a child's self-image and can help to instill a lifelong virtue of empathy, but these lessons should be learned in collaboration with—not at the expense of—a bulldog.

A Pal for Your Other Dog

Puppies are also adept at amusing members of their own species, once those members have come to accept the puppies' presence. If you are acquiring your first puppy, you should think seriously about acquiring two, even if there is always someone at home during the day and your puppy will not have to spend great amounts of time alone. In addition to human company, puppies should enjoy the company of another dog, who will always be interested in romping and stomping long after humans have tired of the game, and who is always more willing to let another dog use him for a pillow than a human is.

If you have a dog already and that dog is still at a flexible age, preferably five years old or younger, it is not too late to add a second dog to the house-

hold, providing you manage the introduction properly (see Introducing Other Pets, page 26). Before you do, though, you should consider certain realities.

Two dogs are not as easy to keep, feed, clean, and look after as one. Nor, in some cases, will you simply be doubling your work load by adding a second bully. That load can increase geometrically, not linearly, depending on the personalities of the dogs involved. But, and this is a significant *but*, whether or not your work load increases by a factor of two or three, the pleasure that two dogs provides is always more than twice as great as the pleasure that one provides.

If you are going to add a second dog—or acquire two dogs at once— you have to decide which of three configurations is going to be most conducive to peaceful coexistence: two males, two females, or one of each. Again, opinions vary. One owner will say that two males are "a lot more 'buddier'" than a male and a female are. Others say that a male and female make a better choice, even though females do tend to dominate males. Still others recommend two females. If you are getting two bullies at once, the breeder(s) of those dogs should be able to help you in this regard. If you already have one dog and you are adding a bulldog to your

Give 'em enough rope and they'll play for hours on end.

but if you are looking for a puppy because your previous dog has died, do not expect the new puppy to be just like your old one. Your new puppy deserves to be loved for who she is, not resented for what she is not.

A Gift for a Friend

"Hearts are not had as a gift, but hearts are earned," wrote the Irish poet William Butler Yeats. The same applies to puppies. Quite simply, puppies are not for giving. It is presumptuous and risky to give someone a puppy, no matter what the occasion. The gesture might succeed occasionally, but more often than not this is an idea whose timing is unfortunate, and the puppy is frequently the one to bear that misfortune.

Breeding or Showing

Breeding a handsome, well-mannered puppy can provide joy, satisfaction, and the feeling of achievement that accompanies any creative endeavor. There is, however, a great responsibility attached to this undertaking. Before you buy a puppy for breeding, you should ask yourself why you want to do so. If your answers include winning fame and fortune in the dog world, perhaps you should consider a hobby that does not involve living creatures. Few breeders become overnight sensations; few litters are filled with nothing but show-quality puppies; and few people make money selling puppies. Indeed, making money is never a valid reason for breeding any animal.

Why Would a Bulldog Want You?

More important than why *you* want a bulldog is the question: Why would a bulldog want you? As important as this inquiry is, especially from the bulldog's perspective, few people think of asking themselves if they would make good dog owners. They spend a lot of time worrying about whether a bulldog will

Bulldogs have been called the sweetest, most courageous canines on earth, and for good reason.

family, the sex and temperament of your present dog should be the guiding criteria.

To Replace a Former Pet

Persons whose dogs have died are often advised to go out and get another dog right away. For some people this is good advice; for others, it is insensitive and insulting. Only you know whether you need time to grieve over the loss of a dog or whether you need a new puppy to take your mind off your grief, shed, whether it will bark a lot, how much grooming it will require, how much it will eat, and whether bullies are as stubborn as some people say they are; but few people ask themselves if they have the right stuff to be a bulldog owner. If you put yourself in a puppy's place—another exercise too few dog owners practice—you might be in a better position to see what it takes to be a good dog owner.

You Have Studied the Breed

Are you interested in a bulldog because you have read about the breed and are attracted by its characteristics? Do you know someone who owns a bulldog that you have always admired? Or do you want a bulldog because you saw one on television or in a movie?

No one denies that attractiveness is often the first step to true love, and no one is going to fault you if you were first drawn to bulldogs because you "thought they were neat-looking." Many a lifelong romance of the two-legged variety began because one or both parties thought the other was pleasing to the eyes. If your affection stops resolutely at the surface, however, you are neither a good prospective dog owner or spouse. Before you buy a bulldog, you should know how the breed originated and what sort of special considerations bulldogs require (see Understanding Your Bulldog, page 53).

Your House Is Air-conditioned

The bulldog is unsuited for the kinds of places that have climates to which people flock to escape the winter. Indeed, the bulldog is built for climates where people go to escape the summer. If your house is not air-conditioned—or if the rooms where your

Hear No Evil, See No Evil, Speak No Evil, and their lawyer.

bulldog will spend warm days are not air-conditioned—your bully will have no place where she can get comfortable. This is not fair to your bulldog, whose breathing apparatus is the victim of fashion.

You Have a Fenced-in Yard

Although bulldogs do not need a lot of exercise, they do benefit from fresh air, a change of scenery, and a chance to gambol about off lead when they are in the mood. Some people think nothing of tying their dogs out in the yard, but you should think twice before doing so. Bulldogs are not lawn ornaments. If they are going to be left outdoors, weather permitting, they should be able to move about freely. They should also have access to shade and fresh, cool water.

Bully for You

There are several questions to be answered before choosing a puppy. Where is the best place to acquire a dog—from a breeder, a pet shop, an animal shelter, or a rescue group? How much should you expect to pay? How can you tell if the dog you like is healthy and has a good personality? Do you want a male or female? A puppy, an adolescent, or an adult? What color would you like? Should you have one dog or two?

Male or Female?

Some people—because of preference, experience, or both—are inclined to select a male or a female dog. Any bulldog, given attention, a supply of things to chew, and a place on the bed at night, will make a fine companion. There are those who will proclaim that females are more hyper or that males are more bumbling, but the point to keep in mind when one of these canine philosophers begins to wax important is this: He or she is most likely talking not about any significant sample of dogs, but merely about the dogs he or she has known from limited experience.

We can say for certain that spaying a female bulldog will cost $30 or so more than neutering a male. Otherwise, there is no difference in the expense associated with housing an altered male or female—and no difference in the amount of care each sex requires.

Why You Should Alter Your Bulldog

Altered dogs make better companions because they are more civilized than dogs that are sexually intact.

Unaltered males, for example, are given to lifting their legs to christen the refrigerator or the lounge chair with urine as a means of marking territory and attracting females. Unaltered males also are inclined to make sexual advances at people's legs and to regard any other dog as a potential mate or sparring partner. Most unaltered females come into season (or heat) twice a year. The indications for this condition are vulvar swelling, blood spots on the rugs, and, quite frequently, unannounced visits from neighborhood dogs who loiter around the back door. The average heat lasts 21 days, but those 21 days will seem longer than the three weeks before Christmas did when you were a child expecting a new bicycle.

There are socially redeeming reasons for altering your bulldog, too. Too many puppies are produced by irresponsible people who are looking to feed their competitive egos, turn a quick profit, or let their children observe the miracle of birth. Such misguided parents should take their children to an animal shelter instead and let them see the downside of the miracle of birth: the euthanasia of homeless dogs, who invariably go to meet the needle with their tails wagging. There is no more disquieting sight in the human–animal "bond" than the moment at which it is severed prematurely.

With millions of healthy dogs being destroyed annually for want of responsible owners, the decision to bring more puppies into the world is not one to be made lightly. For all but a few people it is not one that should be made at all. The pet overpopulation problem cannot be solved by the unrestricted breeding of puppies. The number of dogs killed in shelters each year argues for restraint and common sense on the part of humans, especially those who call themselves animal lovers.

When to Alter Your Bulldog

Dogs should be altered at an age where sexual development is nearly complete, but undesirable traits—urine marking by male dogs, for example—have not become habits. Most veterinarians suggest that this age occurs for females when they are about six months old. Males should be neutered when they are seven to ten months old.

Puppy, Adolescent, or Adult

Bulldog puppies could not be more appealing. They are a beguiling triumph of curiosity over common sense, and what they lack in experience, they more than make up for with their exuberance. They barge joyfully through their food bowls and their owners' lives. They are a snuffling bouquet of puppy breath, a tail-wagging, heads-lolling, eyes-shining experience. They make the most poker-faced among us laugh and inspire the most proper individuals to engage in embarrassing fits of baby talk. The less controlled among us are, of course, toast.

The adolescent bulldog is scarcely less appealing than his younger self, and an adult bulldog is not much different from an adolescent. Indeed, it is difficult to determine where adolescence leaves off and adulthood begins with bulldogs. Therefore, the prospective owner should not feel that he or she must have a puppy. A bulldog of any age is a dog for any season.

Color

According to the American Kennel Club's official bulldog breed standard (see Appendix, page 94), "The various

A litter of bulldog puppies evaluating a potential owner.

colors found in the breed are to be preferred in the following order: 1) red brindle; 2) all other brindles; 3) solid white; 4) solid red, fawn, or fallow; 5) piebald; 6) inferior qualities of all the foregoing. Unless you are going to show your dog, however, any color you like is a perfectly good color for a dog.

One Dog or Two

If you have no other pets and your house is empty during the day, you should consider getting two bulldogs. If buying a second bulldog would tax your budget, adopt a dog—one that is roughly the same age as the bulldog you are purchasing—from a local shelter. Watching two dogs at play is at least twice as much fun as watching only one. Besides, if your bully has a playmate, you will not be required to play that role quite so often. Also, your dogs will be less apt to get bored or lonely if they have company when you are away. Of course, when you adopt a dog from a shelter, you should

Bulldogs are more at home by the hearth.

follow the same guidelines you observe when purchasing one (see The Healthy Puppy, page 14).

Show Dog or Pet

Unless you are planning to show your bulldog or to breed him (see Buying a Show Dog, page 67), you want a pet-quality bulldog. Unfortunately, the designation *pet-quality* has a certain snooty and dismissive-sounding ring to it, but its bark is worse than its meaning. Pet-quality simply means that a dog has some cosmetic liability that argues against his breeding or showing success. Pet-quality bulldogs may not be quite the right color, or they may have muzzles that are too narrow, ears that are too erect, tails that are curved or curly, or some other "fault" or minor constellation of faults.

All of the above are surface defects. They do not in any way detract from the bulldog's nonpareil personality. You cannot judge a bulldog by its color. Every bulldog is a quality dog on the inside.

Where to Find a Bulldog

At a breeder's: The best person from whom to buy a bulldog is a breeder who raises a few well-socialized litters a year. Look for the names of such individuals in dog magazines, in the classified sections of newspapers, on bulletin boards in veterinary offices, in grooming shops and feed stores, and in breed publications (see Useful Groups and Addresses, page 90). Prospective buyers also can meet bulldog breeders by visiting dog shows, which are advertised in newspapers, veterinarians' offices, dog magazines, and, occasionally, on radio or television.

At a pet shop: If you consider buying a bulldog from a pet store, you should ask the owner or the salesperson who eagerly places the puppy in your arms for the name, address, and phone number of the puppy's breeder. If the pet-shop owner is unwilling or unable to provide that information, you should proceed with caution because you are proceeding with less information about the puppy than you would normally have if you were buying from a breeder—unless you found the rare breeder who would not reveal her name and address and who insisted on meeting you in the park with the puppy.

If the pet-shop owner provides the name and address of the puppy's breeder—and if that person lives nearby—you should call or write the breeder and arrange to stop by so that you can observe the conditions in which the puppy was raised and ask any questions you might have regarding the puppy. If the breeder lives far away, you should telephone to ask questions about the puppy that the pet-shop operator might not be able to answer: How many other puppies were in the litter? How old was the puppy when he left his mother? How many dogs does the breeder have? How many litters do those dogs produce in a year? How many different breeds of puppies does the breeder produce? Why does the breeder choose to sell to pet shops rather than directly to the public? You may also want to call the humane association in the town where the breeder lives to ask if the breeder enjoys a good reputation in that community. (In fact, you might want to do this if you buy your dog directly from a breeder.)

By recommending this sort of caution, we do not mean to imply that buying a bulldog from a pet store is more risky than buying directly from a breeder. We do wish to point out, however, that you should find out as much as possible about a bulldog's background no matter where that dog is acquired.

At an animal shelter: One is hard-pressed to imagine that anybody would be less than enchanted with a bulldog. Nevertheless, some bulldogs, through no fault of theirs, do not get along with their owners. In these rare cases, the owner should return the bulldog to his breeder, who should cheerfully take the dog back and find him another, more suitable home—or keep the dog forever, as all reputable breeders will do without fail.

Regrettably, in this less-than-perfect world, some bulldogs wind up in animal shelters with their tails tucked, as far as such is possible, between their legs. If you are willing to wait for a bulldog until one is surrendered at a shelter, visit a shelter and ask to be put on its waiting list.

At a breed rescue club: While you are visiting the shelter, ask if there are any bulldog rescue clubs in the area. Members of rescue clubs often cooperate with shelters by providing foster homes for lost, abandoned, or surrendered bulldogs, feeding and caring for them while trying to locate suitable new owners.

How Much Is That Doggie?

Age, quality, supply, demand, and geography collaborate to determine

Puppies bunched for a goal line stand.

the price of a bulldog. Very young bulldogs, 12 weeks old or so, are generally priced between $800 and $1,500, depending on the breeder's opinion of their potential. An $800 puppy, though his ears may not be correct and his tail may be curved, will make a fine companion if he is healthy and properly socialized. The same is true of a $3000 puppy, whose higher price tag reflects the fact that his breeder believes he has some show potential.

How Old Is Old Enough?

Although new owners are eager to take their puppies home as soon as possible, responsible breeders do not let puppies go until they are at least ten to 12 weeks old. By that age a puppy has been weaned properly, has been eating solid food for several weeks, and has begun to make the transition to adulthood.

Puppies younger than ten weeks old are still babies. Take them away from their mothers and their siblings at that age, and the stress of adjusting to new surroundings may cause them to become sick, to be difficult to house-train, or to nurse on blankets or sofa cushions—a habit they sometimes keep the rest of their lives.

Unfortunately, some breeders are eager to place puppies as quickly as possible, especially those breeders who have many puppies underfoot. Do not let an irresponsible breeder talk you into taking a puppy that is too young.

The Healthy Puppy

A healthy puppy's eyes are shiny, bright, and clear. His nose is cool and slightly damp. His gums are neither pale nor inflamed. His ears are free of wax or dirt. His body is smooth, perhaps a little plump, but not skinny. His coat is free of bald patches, scabs, or specks of black dirt. The area around his tail is free of dirt or discoloration.

A puppy with teary eyes may be in poor health—especially if his nose is warm and/or dry. Pale gums may be a sign of anemia; a puppy with inflamed gums may have gingivitis. Wax in a puppy's ears might simply be a sign of neglect; but ears with caked-on dirt may be infested with ear mites. If a puppy's ribs are sticking out or if he is pot-bellied, he may be undernourished or he may have worms. A puppy with a dull coat or a coat dotted with scabs, specks of dirt, or bald spots may have ringworm or fleas. A puppy whose hindquarters are wet may develop urine scalding. Dirty hindquarters may be a sign of diarrhea. Both urine scalding and diarrhea are signs of potential poor health.

Basic Personality Tests

The basic puppy personality test consists of wiggling a few fingers along the floor about 6 inches in front of the puppy or waving a small toy back and forth about the same distance away. Any puppy that responds to either of these tests by toddling over to investigate you is a good bet for a swell companion—an even better bet is the puppy that rushes over to investigate you before you have a chance to start wiggling your fingers.

Well-adjusted, healthy puppies are curious about fingers, toys, and anything else that moves within sight. Nervous or timid puppies, or those that are not feeling well, are more cautious. Poorly adjusted puppies shrink away from this new phenomenon.

If you have other pets or children at home, the inquisitive puppy is the best choice. The bashful puppy might well make a fine companion, but he may take longer to adjust, and is, perhaps, better left for experienced dog owners who currently are without pets or young children. And the shy puppy? Shy puppies need love, too. In spades. If you have no other pets or if you plan to acquire two puppies at once and you have the time and patience required to nurture such a reluctant violet, you may be the person this puppy needs. If not, perhaps the next person who comes along will be the right owner for this needy pup.

Although temperament is heritable to some degree, the way a puppy is raised is more important in shaping his personality. Bulldogs that are not handled often enough between the ages of three and twelve weeks are less likely to develop into well-adjusted family members than puppies who receive frequent handling and attention during that period. Therefore, you should ask how many litters a breeder produces each year and how many other litters he or she was raising when your puppy was growing up. A breeder who produces more than five litters a year—or who was raising three or four other litters while your puppy's litter was maturing—may not have had time to socialize every puppy in those litters properly. A breeder who raises one or, at most, two litters at a time has more opportunity to give each of those puppies the individual attention he or she deserves. In general, the fewer puppies a breeder produces, the more user-friendly those puppies will be.

Contracts and Papers

When you buy a puppy, you should receive a sales contract from the puppy's breeder. That contract should specify, among other things, the price of the puppy, the amount of the deposit required to hold the puppy, if any, and when the balance of the payment is due. Most contracts also contain a provision stipulating that if at any time the buyer no longer can keep the puppy—or no longer wishes to keep it—the breeder must be given an opportunity to buy the puppy back. If the contract says the breeder will be allowed to buy the puppy back for the price at which it was sold, such a provision could work in your favor if you bought a pet-quality puppy at a pet-quality price. If, however, you buy a show-quality bully at a show-quality price, you should ask that the buy-back clause read "at the going price for bulldogs at the time of resale." By doing so you will be ensuring that you get fair value for the dog in the event that you have put money into showing the dog and it is worth more than it was when you bought it.

Finally, a contract should specify that you have a definite period of time, usually three to five working days after receiving a puppy, in which to take him to a veterinarian for an examination. If the vet discovers any preexisting conditions such as a luxating patella or a heart murmur, you should have the right to return the puppy at the seller's expense and to have the purchase price refunded.

When you give a breeder a deposit on a puppy, be sure to write "deposit for thus-and-such puppy" on the memo line of the check. Make a corresponding notation when you write the check for the balance of the payment. Ask for receipts for all payments made to the breeder. Find out in advance—and in writing if you wish—whether your deposit is refundable in whole or in part if you decide not to take the puppy. Remember, too, that once a breeder has accepted money or some other consideration in return for reserving a puppy for you, he or she has entered into an option contract. At that point the breeder cannot legally revoke or renegotiate the offer. Breeders sometimes try to do this if the puppy begins to develop into a promising-looking dog. Usually, the breeder will graciously offer you another puppy. You do not have to take that puppy. You are within your legal rights to insist upon receiving the puppy that the breeder originally agreed to sell you.

Read all contracts meticulously before signing them. Once it has been signed by both parties, a contract is a legally binding document. If a contract contains any stipulations that you do not understand or do not wish to

Read between the lines before signing any contract to buy a puppy.

15

"All in favor of the motion raise your left ear."

agree to, discuss these issues with the breeder before signing.

In addition to the pedigree and contract, you should receive "papers" when you buy a pedigreed dog. These papers usually consist of a registration slip that you can fill out and send— along with the appropriate fee—to the administrative office of the American Kennel Club (AKC). In return the

Three bulldog puppies in varying stages of wakefulness.

AKC will send you a certificate of ownership.

If you buy a dog or puppy that already has been registered by his breeder, you should receive an owner's certificate that signs the dog over to you. Be sure to check the transfer-of-ownership section on the back of that certificate and to make certain that it has been signed by the breeder. Once you add your signature to that certificate of ownership, you can mail it, with the appropriate transfer fee, to the AKC, which will send you a new, amended certificate of ownership.

Health Certificates

Health certificates and vaccination and deworming records are the most important documents that accompany a puppy to his new home. Do not accept a puppy without these papers. If the breeder says that he or she will send these documents "in a few days," be sure to get an extension, in writing, on the standard three to five days you normally have to get the puppy examined by a veterinarian in order to determine whether the puppy is healthy or whether you have legal grounds for returning it and asking for a refund.

Some breeders, especially those that produce a large volume of puppies, try to save money by giving vaccinations themselves. There is nothing illegal about this practice, yet there is more to immunizing a puppy than drawing vaccine into a syringe and pushing the plunger. Few, if any, breeders are capable of examining puppies as thoroughly as a veterinarian can before administering vaccinations. This examination is important because vaccine given to a sick puppy will do more harm than good. Thus, a puppy should be seen by a veterinarian at least once before he is sold, preferably before his first vaccination.

The First 100 Days

A new presidential administration is often judged on its performance during its first one hundred days in office. Your performance during your first one hundred days with your new bulldog will set the tone for your administration. If you want to look presidential in the eyes of your dog, you should have a legislative agenda and certain items in place before you bring your new bulldog home.

A Shopping List for New Owners

Fax machines and computers have made shopping a round-the-clock experience. If you cannot sleep at night and there is nothing good on television or in the refrigerator, you can spend money until you get sleepy. Thus, there is no excuse for failing to have the requisite supplies on hand when you bring your new bulldog home.

Food and water bowls. The best food bowls are metal or ceramic. Reusable plastic bowls can retain odors even if you wash them carefully. If you choose a ceramic bowl, make sure it does not contain lead, which can be poisonous to dogs.

No matter what they are made of, food and water bowls should be sturdy enough so that a bulldog in a feeding frenzy cannot tip them over easily. They should also be solid and heavy enough not to break, crack, or chip if your bulldog knocks them over. Rubber guards on the bottom of a food bowl will help to prevent it from sliding into the next zip code while your bully is eating.

Place mats. Whether you prefer decorator vinyl place mats or the plain, industrial-strength rubber model, you will extend the life of your carpet or floor if you put something under your bulldog's food and water bowls. This is particularly important if your bulldog eats as if every meal is her last, which is the way most bulldogs eat.

Collar or harness. Most collars are made of nylon or leather. A leather collar looks handsome on an adult bulldog, but a sturdy nylon mesh collar, which is less expensive, is a better choice for a puppy, who will outgrow several collars before reaching his adult neck size. Whatever kind of collar you choose, remember that bulldogs are susceptible to respiratory difficulties if they become overheated. Collars, therefore, should never be tight. The easiest way to check the fit of a collar is by inserting two fingers between the collar and your bulldog's neck. If your fingers fit under the collar easily but snugly, it is adjusted properly. If you have to force your fingers

To keep a choke collar from choking your bulldog, make sure it resembles a letter "P" turned sideways before installing it.

under the collar, get your bulldog a larger collar or let this one out a notch or two.

The choke chain—which is sometimes euphemistically called a check chain—is a controversial item. Some people consider them unduly harsh. Others agree with the bulldog owner who said, "I use a choke collar on my bulldog and do not regret it at all. This kind of collar is the most effective way of training if used properly." Everyone agrees that a choke chain should not be left on a dog after a training session is over.

Some owners prefer to walk their bulldogs in a harness rather than a collar because a harness does not put any pressure on a dog's windpipe. Whether you choose a collar or a harness for your bulldog, do not forget to attach her license and identification tags whenever she leaves the house.

Lead. May be made of leather, cotton, or nylon, and may be of fixed length or retractable. A retractable lead allows you to keep your bulldog nearby when necessary or to permit her to roam more freely in open spaces.

Crate. The crate is you and your bulldog's best friend. A crate provides your bully with a secure place all her own, and it provides you with a feeling of security when you cannot supervise

All hitched up and ready to go.

your bulldog's activities. Until your bulldog is house-trained, you should put her in her crate any time she cannot be with you.

Be sure you buy a crate that will be large enough to accommodate your bulldog when she is fully grown, but small enough so that she will feel cozy in it when she is a puppy. Cover the bottom of the crate with a soft mat equipped with a washable cover.

Food. Some animals eat to live. The bulldog lives to eat. Your bulldog will live longer, however, if she eats right. Food for Thought (page 27) contains a brief but sufficiently detailed discussion of canine nutrition that will enable you to feed your bully wisely.

Grooming tools. Bulldogs are not known for spending large amounts of time fussing with their appearance. Fortunately, you will not have to either, but regular grooming should be a part of every bulldog's routine. Pet-supply shops, mail-order houses, many veterinary offices, and vendors at dog shows carry the brushes, combs, shampoos, nail clippers, powders, ointments, sprays, and other items needed for keeping your bulldog well groomed. Conventional Care and Grooming (page 37) discusses the proper techniques for wielding these implements.

Dog beds. In order to indulge her talents for resting, a bulldog should have access to more than one bed. One of her favorite beds, of course, will be yours; but whether you allow your bully to share that bed is a question for you and her to decide. The bulldog-friendly house, nevertheless, should contain a number of beds in which a bulldog can catch a few ZZZZZs, and make a few in the process. These beds should be set out in the rooms in which you spend a lot of time. This arrangement will allow your bulldog to combine two of her favorite activities: sleeping and being near you.

Dog beds are available in many sizes, colors, materials, and designs. Some are round, some oval, some are made of thinsulate, some are made of medical-grade polyfoam, and some are made in the image and likeness of bean bags. Whatever its construction and design, a dog bed's most important characteristic is a removable, washable cover.

Toys. A brilliant assortment of dog toys—most of them dedicated to the proposition that a chewing dog is a happy dog—await your inspection. The fun quotient is certainly an important consideration in choosing any toy, yet fun is not the sole criterion by which a toy is judged. Toys must be safe as well. Balls with bells inside should be sturdy enough so that a dog cannot get the bell out and swallow it. Before buying a toy for your bulldog, try to imagine how the toy could cause harm. If there is any chance that it could, do not buy it.

Baby gate. Although your bulldog may not think so, there could be times when you want to confine her to a room in which you are not present, once she is house-trained. A sturdy, hinged, swing-open baby gate is essential for those rare times.

Bulldog-proofing Your House

Before you set about bulldog-proofing your house, you should take a few minutes to learn to think like a bulldog. If you really want to get into the role, get down on all fours and crawl about looking for ways to make accidents happen—tinsel on a Christmas tree or a dangling tablecloth, for example.

The leading principle of bulldog-proofing your house is making sure your bulldog cannot reach those objects you do not want her to chew. The second leading principle involves making sure there are closed doors between your bulldog and any room you do not want her to explore. If you

Socket guards should be plugged into your home-safety program.

have sliding glass doors in your house, mark them with tape so your bulldog does not go crashing into them. Make sure all electrical cords are intact. If your dog or puppy is inclined to chew on electrical cords, wrap them in heavy tape or cover them with plastic tubes, which you can buy in an auto-supply shop and some electronics stores. In fact, many owners recommend unplugging all appliances that are not in use if you suspect your bulldog might be developing a taste for electrical cords. Electrical sockets, too, can be a source of surprise to your dog. Cover them with plastic, plug-in socket guards, which you can buy at the hardware store.

Secure cabinets are an invaluable asset in bulldog-proofing your house. Kitchen and bathroom cleansers, chemicals, cleaners, and toilet articles should be kept in cabinets that can be closed or locked securely. The lids on all trash receptacles should be tightly closed. Trash containers with swing-open lids that could be dislodged if your bulldog overturns the containers ought to be replaced. If you sew, be sure to put sewing supplies and yarn away when you are finished using them. And do not leave rubber bands, hot irons, cigarettes, plastic bags, or pieces of string or yarn lying around.

The bulldog's you-got-a-problem-with-that? lower lip is one of its most charming physical characteristics.

Welcoming the Newcomer

After you have filled your shopping cart with supplies, set up the crate, deployed several dog beds throughout the house, and taken one last trouble-spotting stroll around the premises, it is time to bring your new bulldog home. If

"I'm an old cowhand from the Rio Grande, and I learned to ride 'fore I learned to stand."

you work during the week, schedule the welcoming for the start of a weekend or a holiday. Keep in mind that even though you have planned carefully for this day, it will come as a major surprise to your dog—and as an earthshaking event to a puppy. The puppy you bring home will have just left her mother, her playmates, her people, and the only home she ever has known. Most puppies adjust swimmingly—after a while. They bounce their way around their new homes with great excitement and curiosity, delighted to be the center of attention.

Other puppies (and older dogs) may not make the initial transition so smoothly. You should not be surprised, much less insulted, if your new bulldog looks apprehensive. To make your dog feel as comfortable as possible, keep the welcoming party to a minimum. Once your bulldog has taken the measure of your household, she will become more at ease, but that process should be taken one room and one or two family members at a time.

When bedtime arrives, your bulldog is likely to discover for the first time in her life the true meaning of loneliness. Many people suggest that your bulldog will feel more comfortable in her new home if she has something from her former home on hand: a favorite toy, a blanket or bed, or a favorite food. These items give off familiar, comforting smells that are reassuring in a strange, new world. Night time will be less traumatic if you put your bully's crate in the bedroom for a few nights until she gets used to the idea of sleeping in it.

Crate Training

To a dog a crate is a security blanket. Introduce your new bulldog to her crate during her first hours in the house. After you have played with her for a while and have given her a chance to explore the house a bit and

Nothing becomes a natural beauty more than a bouquet.

to have a visit outdoors, place her in her crate with an interesting toy or treat. Leave the door open and stay in the room. (You can also help to establish your bulldog's attachment to the crate by feeding her in it the first couple of times.)

After your bulldog is used to sitting in her crate with the door open, latch the door the next time you put her in the crate. Stay in the room for a minute or two watching television or going about any sort of normal activity. Then let your bully out of the crate and tell her what a good dog she is.

Before long your bulldog will be used to the idea of staying in her crate with the door closed. After she is, leave her alone in her crate for a minute or two. Then return to the room and let her out of the crate, telling her what a good dog she is. (Your bulldog will learn to be relaxed about your comings and goings if you treat her matter-of-factly yourself, starting with the crate-training process, so do not make a big fuss—or any fuss at all—when you leave the room.)

By teaching your bulldog to stay in her crate for progressively longer periods, you are preparing her to use the crate as her bed and safe haven, her own private wolf den. A dog will not soil her bed unless she is nervous or desperately needs to eliminate. Thus, if your bulldog develops positive associations with her crate, you will be able to use it as an aid to house training, and she will have a secure, comfortable place to stay when you cannot supervise her.

If possible, keep your bulldog near you at all times during her first few days in her new home—even if you have to move the crate from its daytime location to your bedroom at night. This will do much to ease your bulldog's adjustment.

This puppy's body language seems to say, "I think it might be time to go out."

HOW-TO:
Introducing the Collar or Harness

If at first you don't succeed, try again tomorrow.

Although bulldog puppies can adjust to a collar when they are seven or eight weeks old, there is no need to introduce the collar that soon. When your puppy is between ten and twelve weeks old, put a collar around her neck when you begin to prepare her meals. Remove the collar just before feeding her. After a few days put the collar on her at other times during the day, leaving the collar on a little longer each time. In about a week add her identification and license tags to the collar.

Introducing a harness to your bulldog is hardly more complicated than introducing a collar. After spending a few minutes playing with or petting your bulldog, set the harness on her back. If she appears uncomfortable—i.e., if she rolls on the floor, scratches at the harness,

and appears to enter a catatonic state—talk reassuringly to her, pet her a few seconds, remove the harness, and try again tomorrow. If she does not seem to mind the harness, hook it up and be done with it. Be sure to give her a treat once the harness is in place. Do not give her a treat if she recoils from the harness. Reas-

surance is enough in that case.

After your bulldog has accepted the harness, leave it on for five or ten minutes a day for several days. Then leave it on for 10 or 15 minutes a day and, finally, for 15 to 20 minutes a day after that.

Lead Training

The lead should be added to the collar or harness in much the same way the collar or harness was added to your bulldog—gradually and in the least obtrusive way possible. Some trainers recommend putting a lead on a dog, allowing her to drag it around a few minutes in order to get used to it, then praising her and removing the lead. Those trainers suggest repeating this routine for several days until a dog is used to the lead.

If you are the kind who installs software without reading the manual first, you may want to proceed directly to step

Most bulldogs will consent to wear a collar, particularly when it means they are going outside.

2: Pick up one end of the lead and hold it. Do not try to walk your dog anywhere, simply hold the lead while she moves about, following her wherever she goes. Remove the lead after three or four minutes.

After several sessions of the bully wagging the leader, you will be ready to have your bulldog follow where you lead. To begin, she ought to be on your left side, your left arm should be held naturally by your side, and the lead should be in your left hand. Turn toward your dog, show her the treat you have in your right hand, and take a step or two forward. If she steps toward the food—and it is the rare bulldog that will not—move forward a few steps. If she follows your lead, give her the treat. If she is hesitant to move, do not drag her. Move the food a little closer. As soon as she moves toward it, say "good," give her the food, and praise her for moving. If she refuses to move, pick her up, carry her forward to the place from which you called her, praise her for being a great dog, but do not give her the treat. Then end the lesson for the day.

Your bulldog should be willing to move a few steps the first day you have her on a lead. On subsequent days, increase the distance she must walk alongside you before she gets her treat.

Pretty is as pretty goes—sweetly in step with her owner.

Conduct these elementary lead training sessions in your driveway or backyard. Do not walk your bulldog in public until she walks calmly and attentively at your side.

Like any new lesson you teach your bulldog, lead training should be taught with large patience in small steps. Although they do not lack intelli-gence, animals often find new experiences unsettling. The easier, more digestible you make the lesson, the more likely your bulldog is to grasp it. And do not forget that pleasing you is one of the most pleasing activities for your bulldog. Your training methods should not raise speed bumps on your bully's road to happiness.

The Secret of House-training

House-training a dog is not rocket science, but the term is misleading because it is you, not your dog, who is being house-trained. As soon as you realize this, you will be ready to master the first—and only—principle of house-training: Your dog will be house-trained as soon as you know she has to relieve herself before she does. Fortunately, this is almost as easy as it sounds. If you understand a puppy's behavior patterns, she can be house-trained with little difficulty and a minimum of floor cleaning.

If your bulldog is not house-trained when you get her, you will have to take her out of doors several times a day. The first trip out occurs immediately after your puppy wakes up in the morning. Make sure she has urinated and defecated before you take her in

Your puppy is house-trained if she tells you she has to go out before she decides to go inside.

for breakfast, and be sure to praise her generously for her achievements.

In addition to her morning walk, your bulldog will need to go outside at least half a dozen other times during the day: ten to 15 minutes after each meal, immediately after waking up from naps, after play sessions, just about any time she has been awake for two hours since the last time she was outside, and whenever she begins sniffing the floor and pacing about in a preoccupied manner. Finally, she ought to be taken outside the last thing before going to bed for the night and, because very young puppies cannot defer elimination for more than four hours or so—at some point during the night until she is three or four months old.

Your puppy may not urinate and defecate every time she goes out, but she ought to do one or the other on every trip if you give her enough time. Do not take her back inside no matter how cold, wet, or uncomfortable you are until you have given her ten minutes to gather her thoughts. If she does draw a blank, put her in her crate with a toy when you get her back in the house, and try her again in 30 to 45 minutes.

As your puppy matures, she will need to go outside less frequently. After she is six months old, she will be eating twice a day instead of three times, so that is one less trip, and she probably will not have to go out right after breakfast if she has gone out just before eating. You will also be able to dispense with the midnight run. Nevertheless, you will have to take your dog outside four times a day, 365 days a year, all the years of her life. If you find that routine inconvenient, get a cat. (Because a puppy's ability to control urination and defecation is limited, you should not acquire a bulldog puppy who is younger than four months old if no one will be available to take her outside during the day.)

When your bulldog has an accident, do not make a federal case out of it, especially if the accident has already occurred. If she begins to soil the house in your presence, just say no in a loud voice, pick her up, and, holding her at a discrete distance from your body, take her outside.

Introducing Children

Kids and dogs are two of this culture's favorite photo opportunities. The ultimate Kodak moment. In real life, however, negotiations between dogs and kids are not always picture perfect. Children who are too young or immature to treat a bulldog properly can be a threat to her sense of confidence. Before a child can be allowed unsupervised interactions with a bulldog, the child must be mature enough to understand that bulldogs do not like to be disturbed when they are eating or sleeping, that there is a right way to hold a bulldog, and that a bulldog's ears and tail are not pull toys. The age at which these lessons can be assimilated varies from one toddler to the next, but as a rule, parents should wait to buy a bulldog or a puppy until their children are roughly four years old.

Even if parents think their children can be trusted to play with a bulldog without trying to mug it, parents should explain that what is fun for children may be painful for the dog. Parents should also explain that children must be careful to watch where they walk and run when the bulldog is around—and that bulldogs can be frightened by loud, unfamiliar sounds. Ask the children to speak and play quietly until the bulldog gets used to them. Caution them not to pick the bulldog up until you feel she is comfortable enough in her new surroundings not to be traumatized by an impromptu ride. Teach children the proper way to hold a bulldog: one hand under her rib cage just behind

A bulldog puppy playing dress-up in an adult suit.

the front legs, the other hand under her bottom, with her face pointing away from theirs. Have them practice this while sitting down in case they

Is it any wonder that bulldogs have been used to sell everything from steel wool to trucks?

25

The new arrival is interviewed by the Head Dog in Residence.

drop the bulldog or she jumps from their arms.

Introducing Other Pets

If you have other pets, do not include them in the welcoming party when you bring your new bulldog home. Confine your cat in a room or put him in a cage if you have one. Put your other dog in his crate. After you have hung out with your new bulldog for a few hours, allow her to meet your dog. If you have more than one dog,

"Nature teaches beasts to know their friends." —William Shakespeare

make the introductions one at a time, but not one right after the other.

The best way to introduce an older dog to a new one is to put the new dog in her crate before letting the old dog into the room. If the older dog sniffs at the puppy in curiosity, but shows no hostility, put a lead on the older dog and let the puppy out of her crate. The less tension there is between the two dogs, the less tension you need on the lead. If your older dog flattens her ears or crouches ominously, tug on the lead quickly with enough authority to keep her from reaching the puppy. Then lead her out of the room and try the introduction again the following day. If the introduction goes well, give each dog a treat, the older dog first, of course, to reinforce their civil behavior.

Before letting your cat in to see the puppy, be sure the cat's claws are clipped. Put the puppy in her crate, then let the two animals sniff at one another. If your cat is lead-trained, put a lead on her when you bring her in to meet the puppy. If not, stay close to her and the puppy. Chances are, a puppy–cat introduction will not go as smoothly as a puppy–dog meeting, but this does not mean your puppy and your cat will not be able to coexist peacefully.

The chances of hostilities breaking out between your new bulldog and your present pets vary inversely with the age and tenure of the cat or dog already in residence. If you have an eight-year-old pet that always has been an only child, you probably should not get a new dog or puppy. If your pet is four years old or younger, you should be able to introduce your new bulldog if you manage the introduction carefully—and if you keep in mind how you would feel if a stranger suddenly was brought to your house for an indefinite stay without your prior approval.

Food for Thought

For reasons not easy to comprehend, chefs enjoy a bubbling celebrity status these days. If you cruise the byways of cable television any afternoon, you are bound to find several cooking shows; and every other week, it seems, the local bookstore is setting out the fine china for some stove jockey, more often overweight than not, with a volume of new or recycled recipes to flog.

The hand that feeds the bulldog is no less a celebrity's than the television chef's. What's more, you do not have to be a gourmet cook or command a gleaming arsenal of expensive cookery to feed your dog a balanced, nourishing diet. Indeed, you do not have to know a dispensable amino acid from an indispensable one—or the number of amino acids a dog requires—to be a good provider. All you need are a few coping strategies. These, of course, you can acquire by reading this chapter.

Dry, Semimoist, or Canned?

Dog food is not hard to find. Supermarkets, convenience stores, pet shops, feed-and-grain emporiums, discount-buying clubs, and veterinarians will gladly sell you all you need; and some of those places will even have someone carry it out to the car for you. The tricky part, and it really is not all that tricky, is sorting your way through the boxes, bags, cans, and competing manufacturers' claims.

Dog food is available in three basic configurations: dry, semimoist, or canned. Dry food is less expensive, easier to store, and more convenient to use than canned food. Dry food also helps to reduce dental plaque to some extent. Canned food is generally more tasty and, because it is 75 percent moisture, is a better source of water than are other foods. (Dry food contains roughly 10 percent water; semimoist contains 33 percent.)

Dry food is the dog owner's favorite. It was sold to the tune of $2.67 billion in 1994, accounting for 52 percent of total dog food expenditures, according to the Pet Food Institute. Canned food was second in popularity, accounting for 23 percent of dog food sales. Semimoist food, because of its high chemical content (preservatives and coloring agents) and its relatively higher price, occupied a much smaller sliver of the dog-food pie—barely 2 percent.

The cook, her hat, the dog, and its dinner.

From a young age the bulldog displays a stoic nature, even when it's up to its chin in studio props.

Generic, Private Label, Regular, or Premium?

Besides having three categories of dog food from which to choose (four, if you include soft-dry food), you can select from generic, private-label, regular, or premium brands. Generic dog foods, which often do not carry a brand name, usually are produced and marketed close to where they are sold, thereby reducing transportation and purchasing costs. If, however, generic foods are produced from cheaper materials, they may not provide the nutritional quality of private label, regular, or premium foods. Before buying a generic or any brand of dog food, look for the nutritional-claim statement on the label and, just to be safe, buy only those foods whose claims of nutritional adequacy are based on Association of American Feed Control Officials (AAFCO) feed-trial procedures.

Private-label foods, which usually bear the house-brand name of a grocery-store chain, may be manufactured by the same companies that produce generic dog food; or they may be manufactured by nationally known companies that also produce their own, more recognizable brands. Instead of the traditional "Manufactured by ___" statement that appears on the labels of generic, regular, or premium foods, private-label brands will contain one of the following statements: "Distributed by ___" or "Manufactured for ___."

Regular brands are foods with nationwide distribution and nationally recognizable names. Manufacturers usually make no special nutritional claims for regular dog foods, beyond, of course, the claims that they are good for your dog, promote strong bones, shiny coats, and healthier teeth, and that they meet AAFCO requirements.

Premium brands command top dollar and are made with top-of-the-line processing techniques that, manufacturers claim, reduce nutrient loss during heating. Moreover, say manufacturers, premium foods, which can cost up to twice as much as regular brands, are made from higher-quality ingredients: chicken necks or backs instead of chicken by-products, such as lung or bone. Finally, premium foods contain few, if any, dyes or additives and, therefore, are less likely to set off food allergies than are regular foods. All this, manufacturers contend, results in foods with taste, smell, texture, and digestibility that are superior to other kinds of dog food.

Some authorities, however, question whether chicken necks are any more nutritious than chicken by-products or that a manufacturer's devotion to better taste, smell, and texture result in more nutritional miles to the gobble. "Higher-quality ingredients and higher palatability do not make premium foods any better than regular foods," says a professor of physiological chemistry at the School of Veterinary Medicine, University of California.

You should also be aware that premium dog foods do not have to meet higher standards than do regular foods. In fact, there is no special definition or standard by which the Food and Drug Administration (FDA) or AAFCO judges premium food.

Devotees of premium foods also claim that their higher digestibility results in lower fecal volume and less fecal odor. The toxicity of fecal odor being in the nose of the beholder, it is impossible to investigate the second of those claims objectively. The lower-fecal-volume claim could be tested, but as one nutritionist has observed, there is little benefit (accrued or otherwise) in scooping up a 60-gram (2.1 oz) dog dropping vis-à-vis a 50-gram (1.8 oz) deposit.

Manufacturers also claim that at the end of the day premium food costs no more than regular food because dogs eat less of premium than they do of regular food. This is one claim that can be tested easily. If you are feeding your dog one can of food a day and that can costs 75 cents and you are considering switching to a premium brand that costs 99 cents a can for the same amount of food, you should be able to feed your dog 75 cents' worth of the premium food—or three fourths of a can instead of the whole can you are presently feeding.

To test this theory, weigh your bulldog on the day you switch to the premium brand. Then weigh him a month later. If he has gained more than two or three ounces, cut back on the premium food. If he has lost more than two or three ounces, you will have to increase the amount of premium food slightly. Needless to say, if your bulldog has gained weight, the premium food costs less per serving than the regular food; but if your dog

Anyone who can resist a bulldog is terminally insensitive to cute.

has lost weight, the premium food costs more.

Making Sense of Dog Food Labels

Reading a dog food label is like squinting at the last line of type on an eye-examination chart. You cannot be certain if you are seeing what you think you are seeing, and even when you are certain, you are reading letters, not words. Letters such as *m-e-n-a-d-i-o-n-e s-o-d-i-u-m b-i-s-u-l-f-i-t-e.* Fortunately, the most significant passage on a dog food label, the nutritional claim made by the manufacturer, is written in plain English.

Nutritional claims come in two varieties. In the first the manufacturer declares that Bowser Bits has been shown to provide complete and balanced nutrition in feeding trials conducted according to AAFCO protocols. In the second kind of nutritional claim the manufacturer attests that Bowser Bits has been formulated to meet the various levels established in AAFCO's nutrient profiles.

Reading a dog food label is elementary when you know how to look for the clues.

In order to make the feeding-trials claim a manufacturer must compare data obtained from an experimental and a control group of dogs, each of which must contain at least eight members. The dogs in the experimental group are fed only Bowser Bits for a specified period of time. The control group is fed a diet already known to be complete and balanced. At the end of the test period, if the dogs fed Bowser Bits do not differ significantly along certain variables from the control group, the manufacturer is entitled to claim that Bowser Bits provides complete and balanced nutrition according to AAFCO's feed-trial protocols. The variables on which the experimental and control groups are compared include weight, skin and coat condition, red-blood-cell count, and other health measures.

In order to make the second kind of nutritional claim—that Bowser Bits was formulated to meet the levels established in AAFCO nutrient profiles—a manufacturer must sign an affidavit stating that he or she (or they)

formulated Bowser Bits from ingredients that will contain, after they have been processed, sufficient levels of all the nutrients AAFCO has determined a dog food should contain.

The difference between buying a dog food that has been tested in feed trials and one that has been formulated to meet AAFCO profiles is like the difference between buying a preferred stock and a futures option: The consumer can be more confident that the preferred stock (the feed-tested dog food) is going to perform the way it is supposed to perform because it has been fed to real dogs in real feeding trials.

The meets-the-nutrient-profiles statement, on the other hand, is somewhat misleading. It does not mean that AAFCO has analyzed the food in question and has certified that it meets AAFCO standards. Nor does the statement necessarily mean that the manufacturer tested the food to determine whether it met AAFCO profiles. This statement simply means the manufacturer formulated the food from ingredients that should have provided enough nutrients to meet the AAFCO profile. We say "should have" because cooking always destroys nutrients in dog food to some extent. Therefore, the nutrients that go into the kettle are always present in greater amounts than the nutrients that go into the can.

Individual state regulators are responsible for checking the validity of nutritional claims. If a food is found wanting, the manufacturer is obliged to reformulate that food in order to provide sufficient levels of the nutrients that were lacking.

Some nutritional claims are conspicuous by their absence. Snack foods and treats (see page 32) do not have to contain any statement of nutritional adequacy. What is more, foods intended for intermittent or supplemental use only must be labeled so and should be used only on an intermittent basis.

Thus far we have discussed only one part of the nutritional claim made on dog food labels: the part that tells you the basis on which manufacturers state their claims. There is, however, a second part to nutritional statements: the part that specifies the dogs for which the food is intended. Thus, a complete nutritional claim for a feed-tested food will say: "Animal feeding tests using AAFCO procedures substantiate that Bowser Bits provides complete and balanced nutrition for all life stages of the dog." A complete nutritional claim for a meets-the-profile food will say: "Bowser Bits is formulated to meet the nutrient levels established by AAFCO nutrient profiles for all stages of a dog's life." Both these statements assure consumers that they can feed an all-life-stages food to their dogs from puppyhood through seniorhood, including motherhood, without worrying.

Instead of being formulated for all stages of a dog's life, some foods are intended for the maintenance of adult dogs only, and other foods are intended to support growth and reproduction. The latter are formulated to meet the increased nutritional needs of pregnant females and puppies. These foods must contain more of certain nutrients—more protein, calcium, phosphorus, sodium, and chloride, for example—than do maintenance foods. (Foods providing complete and balanced nutrition for all life stages of a dog also must meet growth-and-reproduction standards.)

Special Diets

Dogs are put on special diets for several reasons, including illness, old age, or obesity, which often results from lack of exercise. Dogs with hypertension, heart disease, or edema (swelling) should be on low-sodium diets. Dogs with kidney or liver conditions should be fed diets low in protein, phosphorus, and sodium. Dogs that are underweight or that suffer from pancreatic or liver disease should be fed highly digestible food. If any of these or other conditions are diagnosed by a veterinarian, he or she may recommend a special diet. You should follow the veterinarian's instructions faithfully, and, of course, never feed a special diet to a bulldog without first consulting a vet.

In addition to special diets for sick dogs, several companies produce senior-citizen foods for older dogs. These foods are based on two principles: older dogs need less of certain nutrients—proteins, phosphorus, and salt, for example—than do younger dogs; and older dogs are less able to tolerate nutrient excess than are younger dogs.

The jury and animal research are still out on the question of senior foods. It certainly cannot hurt to feed an older dog a senior food—which still must satisfy maintenance requirements in order to make the complete-and-balanced claim—but there is not at present enough evidence to show that senior foods help older dogs in any significant manner.

Other special foods have been formulated to sculpt the overweight dog into a fit-and-trim specimen. Diet dog food, usually called "lite," allows you to feed the same amount of food while lowering a dog's caloric intake. Lite food contains 20 to 33 percent fewer calories than regular food does. Like other special diets, lite food should be fed only to those dogs for whom veterinarians recommend such diets.

Vitamins and Minerals

Dogs cannot reap the harvest from their food without the aid of vitamins, which combine with protein to create enzymes that produce hundreds of

Two good reasons why you should consider getting two bulldogs instead of one.

important chemical reactions. Vitamins also assist in forming hormones, blood cells, nervous-system chemicals, and genetic material.

Although dogs are mostly affected by the lack of vitamins, an excess of vitamins, especially A and D, also can be harmful. Vitamin A toxicity, the consequence of a liver-rich diet, causes skeletal lesions. Vitamin D toxicity, the upshot of unwarranted supplementation, results in calcification of the aorta, the carotid arteries, and the stomach wall.

If a commercial dog food is labeled nutritionally complete and balanced, do not add vitamins or supplements to it. Additional vitamins may upset the balance of vitamins already in the food and may cause vitamin toxicity. The only dogs needing vitamin supplements are those not eating properly because of illness or those losing serious amounts of body fluids because of diarrhea or increased urination.

In addition to vitamins, dogs need the following 12 minerals: calcium, phosphorus, sodium, potassium, chloride, magnesium, iron, copper, zinc, manganese, iodine, and selenium. Minerals help to maintain tissue structure, fluid balance, and the body's acid-base (electrolyte) balance. Because mineral requirements are interrelated, the same warning about vitamin supplements applies to mineral supplements: proceed with caution and only on your vet's recommendation.

Snacks and Treats

There is no more joyous and attentive audience than bulldogs contemplating a treat. Their nostrils flare, their bodies quiver from head to tail, their breath comes in fiery snorts, and their eyes threaten to pop out of their heads.

A considerable subset of the pet food industry is built on this response. Indeed, 20 cents of every dollar spent on dog food is spent on snacks, but dog owners should remember that snacks and treats are nutritionally deficient for full-time use. Moreover, a dog is going to want them full time if you offer them too frequently.

You can feed some foods to your bulldog all of the time and you can

Point, set, game, match to the bulldog.

feed all foods to your bulldog some of the time, but nutritional wisdom is the better part of knowing which time is which. Again, let the label be your guide. If the label says, "Bowser Beef Wellington Bits are intended for intermittent or supplemental use only," then use them intermittently. Do not allow snacks and treats to comprise more than 5 to 10 percent of your bulldog's diet.

Chew Toys

No entrepreneur ever went broke overestimating the dog's fondness for chewing. That is why supermarkets, pet shops, and feed stores bristle with an al dente selection of chewables—all of which are based on the principle that a dog's teeth are certified erogenous zones. If you want to send your bulldog into terminal euphoria, bring home a sweaty, smoked-and-processed pig's ear, set it on the floor, and announce, "Let the gnawing begin." Several hours later your bulldog will have achieved a state of bliss known only to mystics and lottery winners.

Chewables, like any other source of pleasure, also can be a source of pain. Chicken bones should be avoided entirely because they can splinter, get lodged in a dog's throat, or poke holes in his stomach or intestines. (Many bulldog owners who give their dogs marrow or knuckle bones recommend roasting them in a 175°F (78°C) oven for 20 minutes to kill any harmful bacteria.)

Processed cow hide, generally known as rawhide, is the astroturf of the bone world. Long aware of the dog's fondness for chewing, pet supply manufacturers routinely paint, process, and press rawhide into "bones" for a dog's chewing enjoyment. Some rawhide bones are a bleached-looking white, others an off-cream, and still others, which have been basted, broasted, broiled, or roasted, come in colors for

Be sure to monitor your bulldog carefully the first few times you give him a bone or a chew toy.

which there are no words. In addition, some bones are chicken, beef, hickory, cheese, peanut butter, or (for those bulldogs expecting company) mint flavored. Because of its flexibility rawhide also can be fashioned into surreal

Talk about accessorizing—pretty on pink, with nails to match.

approximations of tacos, lollipops, cocktail franks, bagels, french fries, and giant pretzels to appeal to human tastes.

There is the possibility that a bulldog can come to grief by chewing off pieces of rawhide and swallowing them. Be sure to monitor your bulldog carefully the first few times you present him with a rawhide chew toy. If he shows an inclination to chew off pieces of the toy, give him something more substantial to chew on—such as a bone made of hard nylon—instead.

Given manufacturers' ingenuity, one suspects that soon it will be possible to give a dog a different chewable treat every day of the year without giving a treat of the same size, shape, color, and flavor more than once. But whether your bulldog prefers rawhide watermelon slices or marrow bones tartare, all chewables should be served inside the house. A bulldog gnawing happily on a chewy treat in the backyard soon will be attended by a retinue of ants, flies, bees, if they

are in season, and other uninvited vermin.

Water

Water is the most important nutrient needed to sustain normal cell function. Therefore, bulldogs should have fresh water in a freshly cleaned bowl every day. Mammals can lose nearly all their reserves of glycogen and fat, half their protein stores, and 40 percent of their body weight and still survive. The adult bulldog, composed of 60 percent water, is in severe metabolic disarray if he loses 10 percent of his body water, and death results if water loss rises to 15 percent.

How Much and How Often to Feed

The amount of food a bulldog requires is determined by his age, condition, metabolism, environment, biological status, activity level, and ability to convert food into energy and heat. Variations in the effect of these factors among bulldogs can make generalizations, not to mention feeding charts, something of a risk.

If there is one generalization that can be made regarding weight, it is this: The amounts specified in feeding charts on dog food packages and cans are far too generous. Like the manufacturers of soap powder and shampoo, the makers of dog food usually overestimate the amount of their product a person needs to use in order to produce the desired results. The generosity on the part of dog food manufacturers is understandable. They would be embarrassed if dogs were to lose weight on the recommended amounts. Therefore, they recommend high.

During their first year, bulldogs' food requirements diminish somewhat. From the age of three months—about the earliest that a bulldog is likely to be going to its new home—until six

Bulldogs should always have clean water in a clean bowl on a mat to keep the floor clean.

months of age, bulldogs should eat three times a day. Many owners feed their dogs a mixture of dry and canned food, and many breeders recommend that because of a bulldog's propensity for putting on weight quickly and the joint problems that it can cause, bulldog puppies should be fed a senior lite food that is low in protein.

At the three-to-six-month stage, a bulldog should eat about ½ cup of dry food, marinated briefly in warm tap water, and a tablespoon of canned all-life-stages food at each meal. When they are six months old, bulldogs can be fed twice a day, and each meal should consist of ½ cup of dry puppy food, marinated briefly in warm tap water, and a tablespoon or so of canned food. When they are a year old, bulldogs can be fed once a day if that is more convenient for their owners; or, which bulldogs would probably prefer, they can be fed twice daily. Whatever the case, the daily food intake should consist of roughly ¾ of a cup of water-marinated dry food and a tablespoon or two of canned food.

What a Bulldog Should Weigh

It is difficult to venture what any bulldog should weigh without knowing something about its bone structure, muscle development, and height. According to the American Kennel Club breed standard for bulldogs, "the size for mature dogs is about 50 pounds; for mature bitches about 40 pounds": but instead of looking only at the scale to determine if your bulldog exceeds or falls short of its desirable weight, look closely at your bulldog. If you can see its ribs, it is too skinny. If you run your hand gently down its back from shoulders to tail and you feel the spinous processes that stick out along the spine—or if during the same inspection you can feel the transverse processes that protrude sideways from the spine—your bulldog is too thin.

If your bulldog has an hourglass figure or if you cannot feel its ribs readily, it is too fat. Additional bouquets of fat are likely to blossom on the brisket (the area below the chest and between the forelegs), the neck, the abdomen, and the point at which the tail meets the body. If any of these spots seems too well padded, perhaps your bulldog is too well fed. (If you cannot see your bulldog's ribs, but you can feel them without having to squeeze its sides, it is probably neither too fat nor too thin.)

Burdens of Excess Weight

Whether you acquire a 12-week-old flurry of feet and kisses or a mature adult, there is a direct and incontrovertible relationship between what you put into your bulldog's bowl and the quantity of muscle and fat he develops. There also is a relationship between your bulldog's weight and his state of health. Although excess weight is wrongly indicted for causing everything from heart problems to dislocated kneecaps, there is no denying that too much weight is often a contributing factor—and is almost always a complicating one—in many health-compromising conditions.

In addition to aggravating locomotor problems, excess weight makes it more difficult for bulldogs to dissipate heat in sultry weather, a problem already common to all members of the breed, fat or not. Moreover, dogs, like people, are subject to an increasing litany of troubles as they grow older; and bulldogs that are overweight when the specter of old age comes calling are saddled with an unfair handicap in fighting disease and infirmity. It is difficult to specify the point at which a bulldog's health could be compromised by surplus weight, but dogs that are more than 15 percent above their recommended weights are candidates for less food and more exercise.

Switching Diets

When you get your bulldog, find out what kind of food he is used to eating. If that diet, whether commercial or homemade, is both sound for the puppy and convenient for you to feed, continue feeding it.

If you want to switch foods—which you probably will if you buy a puppy that has been raised on a homemade diet and you would prefer to leave the measuring and stirring to the pet-food companies—fold a suitable new food into the puppy's previous food in a one part new to three parts old ratio. Every three or four days increase the new food while decreasing the old until the changeover is complete.

The Joys of Home-cooking

For many people, feeding their dogs is a near-religious experience involving zenlike preparation and adherence to detail. Most home-cookers insist that their dogs would not be as healthy, sparkling, stress resistant, and economical to feed on a commercial diet. They have the economical part right. Ground meat bought from a pet food provisioner is much less expensive than anything that comes in a box, pouch, or can. But whether raw meat—sometimes cooked and always infused with vitamins, minerals, oils, and other molecular talismans—is better than commercial food is questionable. Because meat is deficient in calcium, copper, and vitamins A, D, and E, anyone feeding dogs a diet based on raw meat must add the right vitamins and minerals in the right proportions. This is more complex than pouring calcium, a few tablespoons of vitamins, and some brewer's yeast into the meat and mixing thoroughly. How much calcium must you add to raw meat to restore the calcium–phosphorus ratio to its optimal 1:1 to 2:1 range? How do you convert the 10,000 units of vitamin X per pound listed on the label of a 20-ounce jar of dog vitamins into the proper amount that should be added to a pound of raw meat? Which vitamin additive is the most balanced and complete? Does it also contain the proper minerals in the proper amounts and ratios? And should you cook the meat or feed it raw?

Unless you have some special intuition or knowledge that dog food manufacturers, with their million-dollar research budgets and battalions of feeding-trial dogs, have overlooked, you should leave the nutritional balancing to commercial pet foods. More than 90 percent of all dog owners do.

Conventional Care and Grooming

Enlightened self-interest is one of the principal reasons for grooming your bulldog. Indeed, grooming, like virtue, is its own reward. The more dead hair you remove from the dog, the less you have to remove from the furniture, the rugs, the car, or your clothing.

Although a bulldog's coat is short, bulldogs do shed; and unlike ordinary dog hair, which tends to lie complacently where it falls, bulldog hair weaves its way industriously into any fabric upon which it lands. Once this happens, ordinary vacuum cleaners are powerless against bulldog hair's tenacious grip. Nothing short of a 95-horse-power, industrial-strength, 0-to-60-in-eight-seconds model with dual-quad mud flaps and fuel injection can deal with entrenched bulldog hair that has infiltrated the furniture and rugs.

Time and Tools

You should be able to keep your bulldog and your furniture looking well groomed if you brush the former two or three times a week. Ordinarily bulldogs are not opposed to being groomed and fussed over if you set about the task with the proper reverence and the right tools. Before you begin grooming your bulldog, lay out the implements you will need. Your selection will depend on your purpose: routine maintenance or a close-attention-to-details makeover:

- brush(es)
- flea comb
- cotton balls
- cotton swabs
- lukewarm water
- mineral oil
- toothbrush and toothpaste
- Vaseline
- nail clippers
- paper cup or other receptacle for dead hair

The all-purpose grooming tool for use with a bulldog is a pin brush with stainless steel bristles. Before selecting a brush, test the bristles on your arm. If they cause discomfort, chances

Curry favor with a bulldog by rubbing him the right way when you brush him.

Clockwise from the top: a shedding blade, slicker brush, and pin brush.

are they might on your bulldog, too. Look for a pair whose tips are less pointed or, better yet, covered with plastic.

If you want to be especially thorough about removing dead hair—or if you have several pounds of hair to remove—use a slicker brush or a shedding blade. (The only comb you need for a bulldog is a flea comb, and you will need that only during flea season.)

Grooming Techniques

A well-raised bulldog puppy should be acquainted with the feel of a brush and should not object to being groomed. If brushing is a new sensation for your puppy, you should begin to get her used to that sensation as soon as she is comfortable in her new surroundings. Keep grooming sessions short—five minutes or so at first—and space them two to three days apart until your bully is used to being brushed.

Brushing a bulldog does not require a painter's touch, but there are a few techniques to be mastered. Always brush with the lie of the coat. Do not push down constantly on the brush. Move it across your dog's body smoothly with your wrist locked. Grooming young puppies and some older dogs may require that you wield the brush with one hand and steady the dog with the other. If so, place your free hand on the puppy's chest while you brush her back and sides; or place your free hand, palm up, on her underbelly while you brush her hindquarters or neck.

A bulldog's legs are brushed or combed downward with short strokes. To groom a bulldog's tail, hold it gently by the tip and brush or comb gingerly with the lie of the coat.

As you brush your bully, look for flea dirt, skin rashes, bald spots, and other irregularities in her coat. If you find flea dirt, a flea bath is in order. Skin rashes or bald spots suggest a visit to the veterinarian, who can assess the problem and prescribe treatment.

Do not overlook your bulldog's nose during routine grooming. If your bully's nose looks dry rather than moist and shiny, dab a little Vaseline on it each day until it returns to its normal luster. If you have neglected to do this as needed, apply a coat of Panolog once or twice a day until her nose is repaired.

No More Tear Stains

There is a price to pay for the bulldog's pretty face, and that price is tear stains. These dark discolorations that trouble many short-faced breeds can be the very devil to exorcize once they establish a facehold on your dog. To prevent this from happening, wash your bully's face with lukewarm water and a washcloth each day.

If your bulldog develops tear stains, mix equal parts hydrogen peroxide and white milk of magnesia with enough corn starch to make a paste. Apply this mixture to the stained areas twice a day. After the stains begin to recede (you should start to see results in five to seven days, depending on the severity of the dog's stains), apply the mixture once a day until your bully's face is showroom new again. Be careful not to get any of this mixture in your dog's eyes.

Wrinkle-free Wrinkles

A bulldog's facial wrinkles, which contribute to her angelic appearance, may also contribute to her discomfort—and to a certain dead-fish odor—if they are not cleaned regularly. Wrinkles are like the space between the cushions and the back of the couch. They are landfill in search of debris. Excess food, tears, or other discharges from the eyes accumulate and, subsequently, fester in a bulldog's wrinkles. Those wrinkles must, therefore, be kept clean.

Once a week—or sooner if you notice something fishy about your bulldog's face—hold her head gently in one hand and, with a Q-tip that has been dipped in warm water, clean any dirt or caked tears from her wrinkles. Be sure to wield the Q-tip delicately. Bulldogs are justifiably proud of their faces, and they may take exception to your dredging about in their wrinkles. With patience and bribery, you should be able to overcome their resistance. After you have mined your bulldog's wrinkles, spread a thin application of Vaseline in them with a Q-tip. If you notice bald spots or a rash in your bulldog's wrinkles, take her to the vet to determine whether the dog is growing a fungus.

Ear Care

A bulldog's ears are not difficult to keep clean. All you need to perform this service are a few cotton swabs or cotton balls and some mineral oil or hydrogen peroxide in a small container. Dip the cotton swabs or cotton balls into the oil or peroxide (the choice is

A bulldog's ears must be cleaned gently as a whisper.

yours) and swab the visible parts of the ear carefully. Do not plunge the cotton swab or cotton ball down into the ear canal any farther than the eye can see, or you might do some damage. If you are inspired for some reason to clean your bulldog's lower ear canal, buy a cleaning solution from your veterinarian and follow the instructions faithfully.

Toe Jams

When you groom your bulldog, inspect the areas between her toes to see if she is hatching an interdigital cyst, which is, in reality, an abscess, not a true cyst. This swelling is occasioned when pus forms around a foreign body or loose hair that has insinuated itself into the skin between the toes.

If your bully has an interdigital cyst, treat it twice daily with a mixture of equal parts DMSO gel and Panolog to reduce the inflammation. In addition, make an appointment with your veterinarian to have the hair or foreign object removed.

Clipping Nails

A dog's nails are among the quickest-growing, most indestructible elements in the universe. They should be clipped regularly to help prevent a bulldog from scratching herself, her

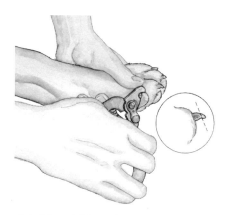

A bulldog might not always agree, but nails have to be trimmed at least every other week.

her toes, and she could suffer a breakdown in the pasterns as a result.

Like all dogs who are not used to having their paws handled—and like a few dogs that are—a bully can turn fussy when you try to clip her nails. This tendency, however, reflects more discredit on breeders who did not begin to clip their puppies' nails early enough than it does on bulldogs themselves. The person from whom you acquire your bulldog should have begun trimming her nails when she was two or three weeks old. If so, your bulldog ought to be tolerant of the process by the first time you approach her with the nail clippers. If she is not so tolerant, you can work on desensitizing her in between nail-clipping sessions by holding her paws or stroking them gently for a few seconds when you are petting her or discussing the day's events with her.

Nail clipping, like death and tax increases, is unavoidable. Treats,

playmates, or her two-legged friends while playing. What's more, if your bulldog's nails are chronically over-long, she will not stand properly on

Bulldogs are supposed to have "rose" ears, i.e., the ear folds inward at the back lower edge while the upper front edge curves over, revealing part of the inside of the ear.

lavish praise, and a determination greater than your dog's should help to make the ritual more pleasant, as will another member of the household who is willing to hold the dog while you clip. Some bulldog owners recommend putting the dog on a table for this exercise; others recommend having someone hold the bully in his or her lap. The idea is to play the game on your court rather than the floor, where the bulldog is liable to think she has homecourt advantage.

Be careful to clip the hooked part of the nail only. Avoid cutting into the quick, the vein inside the nail (see illustration on page 40). Have some styptic powder handy in case you do cut into the quick and it begins to bleed. Dip a Q-tip into the styptic powder and apply it to the bleeding nail. Convey your apologies to your bulldog—but try to stop short of actual groveling—while the blood coagulates. Be sure to give her a treat afterward.

Originally bred for fighting, the bulldog is presently constituted more for comfort than for combat.

A tisket a tasket, bulldogs make good mascots; that's why 38 colleges and universities call themselves "the bulldogs."

HOW-TO:
Bathing Your Bulldog

Before placing your bulldog in the tub, make sure the spray attachment is firmly in place and check to see that you have laid out the implements you will need for the bathing ceremony. These include:
- regular or flea shampoo
- brush(es)
- cotton balls
- Q-tips
- several bath towels
- mineral oil in a squeeze bottle
- hair dryer (optional)

Bulldogs enjoy being fussed over at bath time.

A rubdown after a bath will help to soak up excess water.

Clean your bulldog's ears if necessary (see above) before placing her in the tub. Put a small wad of cotton into each ear to prevent water from reaching the ear canal and possibly causing infection. Put a few drops of eye ointment into her eyes to protect them from stray shampoo. (If your bulldog's face needs washing, do that, too, before you bathe her.)

Put a rubber mat or a bath towel in the bottom of the tub to provide secure footing for your bulldog. Turn on the water and adjust the temperature, testing it with your wrist. If the water feels too warm to you, chances are your bulldog will not care for it either. Adjust the water temperature until it is comfortably warm, and do not neglect the house temperature, which should be at least 72°F (22°C).

If you are giving your bulldog a flea bath, wet her neck thoroughly as soon as you put her in the tub and then apply a ring of flea shampoo to her neck, lathering well. This will help to prevent the fleas on her body from escaping to her face in order to avoid extradition. Next, wet down the rest of your bulldog thoroughly, then apply shampoo, working up a generous lather. Leave the shampoo in the coat for whatever length of time the manufacturer recommends before rinsing. Never lather past your bulldog's neck or you risk getting shampoo into her eyes. If you are using a regular shampoo, rinse your bulldog immediately after lathering.

After your bulldog has been lathered and rinsed—you are finished rinsing when the water coming off your bulldog is as clean as the water going onto her—remove her from the tub and wrap her in a towel. Use another towel (or towels) to dry her more thoroughly. Because baths can have an energizing and, sometimes, a cathartic effect on dogs, take your bulldog outside for a quick run after toweling her dry.

An invigorating dash around the yard is an essential post-bath ritual.

The Healthy Bulldog

There is no substitute for the counsel of a good veterinarian. No book or magazine article, no newsletter, long-time breeder, or Internet forum is a substitute for the diagnosis and prescription provided by a living, breathing, qualified, in-the-flesh veterinarian with his or her hands on your dog. Thus, when your bulldog does not appear well to you, call your veterinarian first, tell him or her the symptoms that look troubling to you, and schedule an appointment if the vet feels it is necessary. Do not phone the breeder first, do not go rifling through textbooks or back issues of magazines, and certainly do not go logging on to some chat group on the Internet for advice. All those sources, like the chapter you are reading now, are simply a way of giving you an idea of what certain ailments look like and letting you know that your dog is not the first one in the world to look ill. They are not a substitute for competent diagnosis and treatment, and they should not be your first recourse in any sort of medical situation.

There are a lot of people—most of them dog breeders—who will tell you that veterinarians do not know and/or appreciate purebred dogs, especially bulldogs, and that vets are more often part of the problem rather than part of the solution. If you are ever trapped in such a conversation, smile politely, listen for as long as you think civility requires, then head for the nearest exit.

If Symptoms Persist

Frequently the first suggestion that a bulldog is unwell is a lack of interest in food. If your bully misses a meal or makes a faint, uninspired pass at his plate but seems to be in good health otherwise, there may or may not be cause for concern. If he passes up two consecutive meals, call your veterinarian, who probably will want to know if your bulldog's temperature is elevated or if he displays additional symptoms of potential illness such as vomiting or diarrhea.

A Brief Veterinary Checklist

Lack of interest in food is not the only, or always the first, sign of illness. You should call your veterinarian if the answer is yes to any of the following questions:
• Is your bulldog's breathing labored?
• Has he been coughing, gagging, or sneezing?
• Is he drinking more water than usual?

"How am I doing, doc?"

- Has he been shaking his head frequently?
- Are his eyes runny, cloudy, or bloodshot?
- Is his nose runny?
- Are his gums inflamed?
- Is his breath foul?
- Has he been digging at his ears?
- Does he have a swelling or an abscess on his body?
- Is he scratching, licking, or chewing himself excessively?
- Is there a large amount of flea dirt in his coat?
- Have you noticed worms in his stools?
- Is there blood in his urine or stools?
- Has he been favoring one leg when he walks?
- Is he dragging his hindquarters across the floor?
- Has he been lethargic for any length of time?

Do not worry about making a pest of yourself by calling your veterinarian whenever your bulldog does not seem right. No concerned vet will be put out by hearing from a concerned owner, no matter how slight the symptom(s) he or she is reporting. And do not hesitate to seek another opinion if you have any reservations about the way your veterinarian is treating your bulldog. (This, perhaps, is the time to consult your breeder or your Internet connections for advice about seeking a second opinion.)

Vaccinations

Until they are roughly six to eight weeks old, puppies are protected from certain diseases by antibodies in their mothers' milk, as long as their mothers have been immunized properly against those diseases and possess sufficient antibodies to confer immunity. Because this passive immunity interferes with the ability to produce antibodies in response to vaccination, puppies are not vacci-

A bulldog's wardrobe ought to include at least one dressing gown.

nated for the first time until they are at least six weeks old.

The vaccine given to puppies contains antigens that have been derived ultimately from viruses or bacteria obtained from live animals. Typically, a six-week-old puppy is vaccinated against distemper, hepatitis, parainfluenza, parvovirus, and leptospirosis. In areas where the bacterial disease leptospirosis is not a problem, veterinarians may vaccinate against corona viruses instead. Whatever the case, the antigens representing these diseases are usually administered in a single vaccine.

When those antigens begin circulating in the puppy's bloodstream, they are detected and seized upon by specialized cells that are part of the body's immune system. After a series of complex evolutions, the puppy's immune system produces cells that

45

are able to detect and destroy the diseases represented by the antigens in a vaccine. Thus, if a dog vaccinated against distemper was later exposed to the virus, distemper antibodies would recognize and exterminate any free-ranging distemper virus particles at large in the bloodstream. And if the distemper invaders managed to infect some of the dog's cells, those infected cells would be recognized, destroyed, and shown the door by other specialized cells in the immune system.

One vaccination, however, does not confer instant immunity on a puppy. Not for five to ten days will a puppy's immune system start to forge a response to the challenge posed by the antigens in a vaccine. That response is low grade and not entirely effective. What's more, one can never be certain how long a puppy's passive immunity will continue to compromise his ability to manufacture his own antibodies, For these reasons all veterinarians revaccinate a puppy in three to four weeks, and many veterinarians re-revaccinate four weeks after the second vaccination. After that, dogs should receive booster shots once a year because antibodies decrease in number over time and the immune system needs to be stimulated to produce additional disease-fighting troops.

The initial rabies vaccination is administered to dogs when they are three months old. Most veterinarians boost that shot when a dog is a year old and then boost it periodically thereafter.

External Parasites

Parasites are living organisms that reside in or on other living organisms (called hosts), feeding on blood, lymph cells, or tissue. Internal parasites dwell inside their hosts. External parasites live on the surface of their hosts.

The external parasites for which a bulldog could be a mobile hotel include fleas, ticks, flies, lice, larvae, and mites. This freeloading collection of insects and arachnids, in addition to damaging skin tissue, may transmit harmful bacteria and menacing viruses to your bulldog. In significant quantities external parasites can sap your bulldog's energy, weaken his resistance to infection and disease, and endow him with a number of diseases and/or parasitic worms.

The presence of external parasites is usually revealed by flea dirt, skin lesions, pustules, hair loss, itching, redness, dandruff, scaling, scabs, growths of thickened skin, or an unpleasant odor. If you notice any of these symptoms while you are grooming your bulldog or if he begins to scratch or bite at himself excessively, call your veterinarian. She or he will prescribe treatment. The earlier that external parasites are detected, the easier they are to rout. This, among other reasons, is why you should groom your bulldog two or three times a week.

Humans, too, can be affected by some of the external parasites troubling their dogs. If flea infestation is severe enough, fleas may hop onto humans for the occasional take-out service. Certain kinds of mites will migrate to humans, too, and so will ticks. Especially worrisome to humans are ticks that carry Rocky Mountain spotted fever and Lyme disease. The latter is the most common tick-borne disease in the United States.

Bulldogs afflicted with external parasites will have to be treated with parasiticidal dips, powders, ointments, and/or shampoos. Always follow your veterinarian's instructions when using these products.

Waging War on Fleas

Eternal vigilance is the price of a flealess bulldog. There are many shampoos, sprays, powders, mousses, bombs, roll-ons, drop-ons, flea collars, and dips designed to kill fleas. One of the most recent additions to this arsenal is a pill taken monthly that does not kill fleas, but prevents the eggs that females lay from ever becoming adults. Another recent development, a liquid that is spread in a small amount each month between the shoulder blades, kills fleas on contact. Before using any of these flea fighters, consult your veterinarian and use them according to instructions.

Insecticidal flea collars do not light up the scoreboard with flea kills, and some dog owners are concerned about the harm done by pesticides in these collars. If you choose to put a flea collar on your dog, remove the collar from its sealed package and snap it taut a few times to shake off excess insecticide. Wash your hands immediately. Let the collar air out (away from pets and children) for 24 to 36 hours before putting it on your bulldog. Watch him closely for several days to be sure no sores appear. If they do, if the dog seems groggy, or if he develops nasal irritation or inflamed eyes, remove the collar at once. Collars that get wet must be removed and dried. Many collars are no good once they are wet, and should be discarded.

Additional weapons in the war against fleas include ultrasonic flea collars, food-grade diatomaceous earth (sold in hardware stores and garden-supply centers), and various vitamins and oils. Ultrasonic collars do not sound like much of a threat to fleas. A study conducted at the School of Veterinary Medicine, Purdue University, evaluated two brands of ultrasonic flea collars. Each was tested on a group of five cats for a seven-day period. During that period cats in a control group wore no collars. At the end of the study, cats that had worn ultrasonic flea collars were still wearing 98.6 percent of their fleas. Cats that had not worn collars retained 97.4 percent of their fleas.

Diatomaceous earth is sprinkled into rugs and upholstery because its sharp surfaces puncture a flea's armor. Salt and 20 Mule Team borax are also used because they cause fleas to dry up and die upon contact. Brewer's yeast is added to a dog's food and dusted into his coat and bedding. Garlic is added to food; vinegar to a dog's drinking water. Chelated zinc, lecithin, cod liver oil, cold-pressed, unsaturated vegetable oil, kelp, and Vitamin C also are touted as flea remedies. Most scientists and veterinarians, however, are skeptical about the value of such remedies.

Internal Parasites

Protozoa and worms are the internal parasites to which a bulldog could be host. Protozoa are usually one-celled organisms that may contain specialized structures for feeding and locomotion. One protozoan sometimes found in dogs is *Toxoplasma gondii,* which is carried in oocysts shed in cat feces. If you have a cat, do not allow your bulldog to go truffle hunting in the litter box. Fortunately, the threat of your bulldog's being infected by *T. gondii* from your cat is limited. Once a cat's immune system responds to *T. gondii,* the cat stops shedding oocysts. (Coccidia, another protozoan disease, is usually found in young dogs kept in crowded conditions.)

The presence of three kinds of worms that infest dogs—roundworms, hookworms, and whipworms—can be detected through stool-sample analysis. Tapeworms, however, elude this method of identification. They are best detected by the ancient Egyptian technique of peering studiously at a dog's anus. During this examination, the inspector is looking for small, white

Conscientious owners do not allow poor dental hygiene to put the bite on a dog's health.

tapeworm segments that look, you will forgive the indelicacy, like rice. These segments also can be seen on freshly minted stools.

The presence of heartworms can be detected by blood-sample analysis. If your bulldog is negative for heartworms, your veterinarian can prescribe preventive heart-worm medication to keep him that way. If your bulldog tests positive for heartworms, he will require treatment that may include hospitalization and/or surgery.

Never use human toothpaste on your bulldog's teeth.

Most worms, despite their repugnance, are not difficult to control. When you acquire a bulldog, ask the person from whom you get him when he (the bulldog) was last dewormed and what deworming agent he was given. To be safe, take a stool sample and your new bulldog's previous deworming history to your veterinarian. He or she will recommend a safe, effective deworming agent and will set up a deworming schedule.

Pearls Before Teeth

Clean teeth, in addition to being things of beauty and a joy, one hopes, forever, may help to prevent certain diseases of the heart, liver, and kidneys that are thought to be caused by the spread of bacteria from a dog's mouth. Diligent bulldog owners, therefore, do not allow poor dental hygiene to put the bite on their dogs' health.

Dry dog foods, which ought to comprise the bulk of a bulldog's diet, help to a certain extent to reduce plaque—the sticky combination of bacteria, food particles, and saliva that is constantly forming and hardening on a bulldog's teeth. Unfortunately, dry foods are not an unalloyed dental blessing. The carbohydrates in dry foods stick to the teeth and act as compost for the bacteria that is plaque's main ingredient. (Canned dog foods do nothing to remove plaque. What's more, the sugar they contain adds to its buildup.)

Bulldogs are willing to assist in their own dental care by chewing on rawhide bones, knuckle bones, marrow bones, or bones made of hard nylon. Encourage this participation by allowing your bulldog to floss with some kind of bone or specially designed teeth-cleaning toy once or twice a week.

If plaque is not removed regularly from your bulldog's teeth—by you or by your bulldog—it hardens into calculus (tartar) and intrudes itself between the teeth and gums, creating a tiny sinkhole in which bacteria multiply. These bacteria invade the gingiva (gum), causing it to become inflamed, to swell, and to bleed when probed. This condition, known as gingivitis, is reversible if treated early in its development. If not, it escalates into periodontitis: ulceration of the gums and erosion of the alveolar bone, which holds the teeth in place. Periodontitis is not reversible, and if it is not controlled, the gums and alveolar bone eventually become so eroded that the teeth fall out.

Winken and Blinken about to nod off.

To check for signs of gingivitis, gently but firmly hold your bulldog's head with one hand and lift his upper lip along one side of his mouth with the other hand. Look closely at his teeth and gums. Repeat this procedure on the opposite side and in the front of his mouth. Then inspect his bottom teeth in the same fashion. If there is a red line along his gums, make an appointment to have your veterinarian check your bulldog's teeth.

Other signs of oral disease include morning breath around the clock, avoidance of dry food, resistance to being stroked on the muzzle, brown or yellow crust on tooth surfaces, loss of appetite, and drooling. If your bulldog exhibits any of these symptoms, call your vet and describe the dog's behavior.

You can assist your bulldog in keeping his teeth clean by brushing them once or twice a week. Introduce this idea gradually by having a look at your bulldog's teeth each day. Check them out as you did during the gingivitis inspection, but in addition to just looking, rub a finger along his teeth, first in front of them and then behind them.

When your bulldog is used to this intrusion into his personal space, substitute a soft-bristled children's toothbrush or a finger brush made

especially for dogs in place of your own finger. You will want to add toothpaste to whatever brush you choose. Your veterinarian will be able to recommend a suitable toothpaste.

Never use human toothpaste on your bulldog's teeth. The foaming agent it contains can cause gastric problems in dogs. Avoid using baking soda or salt to clean your bulldog's teeth. These products do not remove plaque effectively, and they contain sodium, which can be harmful to older dogs with heart disease.

Contrary to folk wisdom, bulldogs do not have locking jaws.

HOW-TO:
Flea-bombing Your House

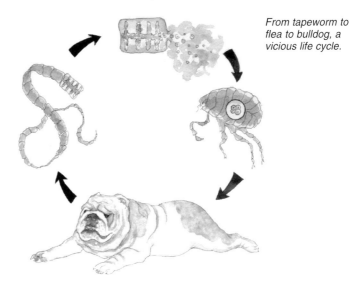

From tapeworm to flea to bulldog, a vicious life cycle.

Fleas are older than dirt and uglier than sin. These blood-sucking machines are armor plated, bad to the bone (figuratively), and able to leap 150 times their own tenth-of-an-inch length, vertically or horizontally. And if you want to talk stamina, one rat flea was clocked jumping 30,000 times without stopping.

Fleas can survive months without eating, and they are able to remain frozen for a year, then revive and conquer. As same-day couriers for bubonic plague, they have taken out more people than war itself: roughly 40 million people from the years 541 to 741, another 25 million in Europe alone between 1347 and 1352, and 6 million in India during one decade from a plague that came out of China in 1855

This bulldog owner is determined to win the war on fleas.

and still lingers in parts of the world today.

Considering the flea's number and nastiness, it is obvious that if your bulldog and your house become infested with fleas despite your diligent efforts to the contrary, you

will need to launch a major offensive to reclaim the lost territory. Simply giving your bulldog a flea bath will not do. If you are treating only the fleas on your bulldog, you are treating only 10 percent of the problem. The other 90 percent is hopping merrily about your house, looking for a meal on which to land.

On the day you have designated as B-Day, leave your bulldog at the veterinarian's for a flea bath and dip, which you will, of course, have scheduled in advance. Leave all your other pets with the vet, too, and be sure to cover any fish tank(s). When you return home, vacuum the house obsessively. Vacuuming is important because carpets, furniture, baseboards, bedding, cracks in the floor, and your bulldog's favorite resting places are the staging areas where flea eggs, larvae, and pupae (the other 90 percent of your flea problem) develop. Flea eggs, four to eight hundredths of an inch long, incubate for 2 to 12 days. Then they hatch into larvae—tiny, white, bristled worms that feed mainly on fecal casts from adult fleas. (Great-sounding family, eh?) After growing—and molting twice—over a period of 9 to 200 days, larvae molt one more time, turning opaque, becoming quiescent, and spinning a loose, whitish-gray cocoon in which they remain for seven days to a year.

Put naphthalene crystals or crushed mothballs in the vacuum cleaner bag or else it will become a traveling flea incubator. When the vacuum bag is full, seal it tightly and bury it in the nearest toxic waste dump. Failing that, put it in an outdoor trash can with a tight lid.

Some persons fear that toxic fumes are released when vacuums are run with mothballs in their bags. If you share this concern, throw the bag away or empty it after each use. Either way, when when you have finished vacuuming, wash all your dog's washable bedding.

Next, close all the windows in the house and set off aerosol foggers in every room. The best bombs to burst in air are the

For maximum effect stand all sofa cushions on end before detonating the flea bomb.

ones that contain IGRs (insect growth regulators), which prevent immature fleas from maturing. Then spray the grass and shrubbery around the house with an insecticide. (Some people spray their yards periodically throughout the flea season.) Then go out to eat.

When you return home, open the windows throughout the house and allow the rooms to air out. Do not bring your bulldog back home sooner than the instructions on the bomb labels recommend. If there is no recommendation of this sort on the label, consult your veterinarian. You may have to leave your bulldog at the vet's overnight

and bring him (the bulldog) home the next day.

Once your bulldog has been bathed and dipped and the house has been bombed, continue vacuuming and fleacombing daily. Fleas removed from your dog can be drowned in a dish containing a little detergent, or they can be crushed gleefully by fingernail. If you see a lot of fleas during your daily combing, dip the dog again the next weekend. If you are not taking any fleas off your dog, it is probably safe to vacuum every other day. If the fleas return en masse, you will have to repeat the B-day flea offensive.

"Hey, I thought you said we were getting bunk beds."

Medicating and Feeding a Sick Bulldog

Ignorance is bliss when medicating a bulldog. As long as the bulldog remains ignorant of the contents of the mound of baby food you offer on a tablespoon or on the tips of your fingers, the pill hidden in that mound of food should go down blissfully. If your bulldog is too sick to eat, pills may have to be administered manually or with a pill gun. The latter is available in a pet shop or from a pet-supply catalog (see Useful Groups and Addresses, page 90). Either way the technique is the same: placing the pill as far back on your bulldog's tongue as possible, holding his mouth shut, and stroking his throat until he swallows. Do not forget to praise him when he does.

Bulldogs convalescing from an illness or injury must consume enough fluid to replace that which they lose through elimination and panting. If your bulldog is unwilling to drink, you will have to get nourishing liquids—water or broths—down his throat one way or another.

Spooning fluid into a bulldog's mouth can be messy and uncomfortable for you and your dog. A syringe or a spray bottle is a better choice. Your veterinarian can tell you how much fluid your bulldog should receive daily.

If your bulldog is off his feed, switch to an all-canned-food diet and warm the food slightly in the microwave to release its aromas before giving it to him. Be sure to stir the warmed food and to test it for pockets of heat before offering it to your bulldog.

When a bulldog is not eating, virtually any food is nutritious food for the time being. Baby food, turkey or chicken from the deli, canned dog food marinated in beef or chicken broth, hamburger seasoned with garlic, broth straight up, anything that will revive your bulldog's interest in eating. (In serious cases you may have to feed your bulldog a pureed diet with a large syringe.)

Understanding Your Bulldog

One otherwise uneventful day in August 1996, Carrboro, North Carolina, Police Captain John Butler got a call from his wife. "Rock ate a car," she said.

The Rock in question was Butler's three-year-old, 65-pound, red bulldog. The car was a blue 1996 Geo, weight undisclosed, being driven at the time by one of Butler's neighbors. Even though Rock had inflicted $1,000 damage on the car with his teeth, Butler did not want people to get the wrong impression about bulldogs.

"They're big babies," he told the *Chapel Hill Herald*. "They love to be petted. They do stupid, entertaining things.

"These dogs were bred for bull-baiting in medieval times," Butler explained. "They would latch onto a bull's nose and hang on until the bull was exhausted."

Butler also assured the *Herald* that Rock had meant the car no harm. "As soon as the guy stopped," said Butler, "Rock stopped chewing on the car because he thought he was going to get a ride. He's not a vicious dog."

Vicious? No. Optimistic? You might say. How many people are going to open the door for a 65-pound dog with his teeth in the quarter panel? Bulldogs, bless their fun-loving hearts, certainly have a keener sense of the absurd than most people do.

With Baited Breath

As Butler correctly noted, the bulldog was bred originally to participate in bull-baiting, a strange and savage ritual that was popular in England from the 13th through the early 19th centuries. "Bulls were baited," according to one Oxford historian, "by being tethered to a stake and then attacked by dogs, usually in succession, but sometimes all together. The dog would make for the bull's nose, often tearing off its ears or skin, while the bull would endeavor to toss the dog into the spectators. If the tethered animal broke loose, scenes of considerable violence ensued." If the bull did not break free, one of the dogs invariably put a lip lock on the bull's muzzle and held on until the bull was immobilized.

The bulldog's strong will and firmly held opinions make him well suited for the director's chair.

Bull-baiting was one of the British national pastimes, "a sport the English much delight in," wrote John Houghton in 1694, "and not only the baser sort, but the greatest ladies."

Aside from its obvious sporting appeal, bull-baiting was considered necessary to drain the bull of poisoned blood and to tenderize its meat. The British, understand, took their beef seriously. By the 17th century beef was a staple in Britain, and a person was not to be considered a glutton, explained John Weemse of Scotland in 1632, if he ate merely three pounds of beef a day, often spit-roasted and noticeably underdone.

Those Mists of Time

The dogs used to tenderize British beef were a rugged lot. Their ancestry, like that of many breeds, contains more speculation than substance. Certain observers believe the bulldog was the parent of the mastiff. Others claim the bulldog resulted from crosses between mastiffs and Dutch pug dogs. According to the majority opinion these days, the mastiff and the bulldog descend from a common ancestor known as the Alaunt. The Alaunt resembled the mastiff and was used by butchers to assist in bringing oxen to their stalls and keeping them there.

Whatever its origin, there is no speculation regarding the bulldog's courage, tenacity and virtual lack of pain receptors. As one writer has commented, "The British bulldog was the most valiant beast the Almighty (assisted by a number of sadistic breeders) had chosen to create." That dog, whom the writer also described as a "devil incarnate," appeared to have outlived his usefulness when bull-baiting was finally outlawed in England in 1835. Fortunately, a number of devotees of this courageous dog decided that its other assets were worth preserving.

What Price Salvation?

The efforts to preserve the bulldog, some people argue, were a mixed blessing whose consequences did nothing for the breed's vitality. This argument was proposed as early as 1927 by Edward Ash in *Dogs: Their History And Development*. "When bull-baiting ended," wrote Ash, "the dog was bred for [the] 'fancy,' and characteristics desired at earlier times for fighting and baiting purposes were exaggerated so that the unfortunate dog became unhappily abnormal. In this translation stage, huge, broad, ungainly heads were obtained, legs widely bowed were developed and frequently the dog was a cripple."

The bulldog's wrinkles, intended to channel the bull's blood away from the bulldog's eyes, were greatly overemphasized. The layback of the face, which allowed bulldogs to breathe while they hung on to a bull's nose, was also exaggerated; and the loose skin on the body, designed to protect the dog's internal organs, grew even more loose.

The conditions described by Ash 70 years ago continue to shadow the bulldog today on both sides of the ocean. The British, of course, are more apt to take those conditions personally. "The bulldog of the 1800s was a potent symbol for our former imperial might," said Marcus Scriven in London's *Daily Mail*. "It was a brave fighter, with a longer muzzle than today's breed and possessed of a muscular agility second to none.

"Now, though, in what seems an inescapably apt metaphor for our decline, the British Bulldog is in dire trouble. [It] suffers eye problems, congenital heart conditions, dental and skin disorders and vertebrae deformities. Its shorter muzzle has led to breathing difficulties, and the large head means pups have to be born by Caesarean section."

The Bottom Lines

To be sure, the bulldog is not for everyone. If you are looking for a long-term relationship, you should realize that bulldogs are not famous for their longevity. The typical bulldog seldom lives beyond 10 years. Nor is the bully the dog for you if you want an obedient dog that will salute on command. Bullies are intelligent, but like many intelligent people, they are apt to trust their own intelligence as much as they do yours. This leads some people to say that bullies are stubborn. Finally, you should know that while they are alive, bulldogs are likely to occasion higher medical expenses than the average breed because bullies are prone to a number of afflictions.

But if you could not help but love a dog that will interrupt your afternoon nap by dropping a bone on your chest—then return with a roll of toilet paper still attached to the holder if you ignore him—your prayers have been answered.

More than a few people have found those attributes and more in their bulldogs, and for all the challenges they present to their owners, bullies remain a popular breed. In 1995 the bulldog added 12,092 new registrations to the rolls of the American Kennel Club (AKC). This figure placed the bulldog 30th in terms of new registrations for the year among the 140 breeds then recognized by the AKC. Just about one out of every one hundred dogs registered that year was a bully, making this dog literally one in a hundred. Bulldog owners, of course, would add several zeroes to the second figure.

They would also, no doubt, second the opinion of the British bulldog fancier who declared that "basking in their owner's love, [bullies] are the happiest creatures alive."

Bulldog owners, basking in their dogs' love and various sound effects, insist that if people were more like

Despite their rugged, all-terrain appearance, bulldogs wilt rapidly in the heat.

bulldogs, the world would be a better place. A rugged civility would reign in place of crabbiness; tenacity would dispatch timidity; loyalty would not be based on self-interest; people who snored would have a ready cover; kids would have a ready playmate; and honesty would be a virtue, not a policy. Indeed, the bulldog fancier believes that the world would be a better place if all *dogs* were more like bulldogs. Chances are you will come to the same conclusion not long after your bully takes over your house and your heart.

Exercise

Bulldogs, being the civilized and sensible creatures they are, do not require much exercise. They do enjoy being outdoors, however, and if at all possible should be provided with a securely fenced yard in which they can trundle about when the spirit moves them. They do not have to spend large amounts of time in the yard. An hour in the morning and another in the afternoon, temperature and/or weather permitting (with access to fresh water, of course) are sufficient. Bulldogs that live

According to one observer, the bulldog's massive head helped to lessen the dog's chances of having its back broken if it was shaken by an angry bull during bull-baiting.

exercise needs are a case in point. Hot or humid weather are a challenge to a bulldog's respiration system, which has been compromised rather severely for the sake of its pretty face. Bulldog owners, therefore, should have an accurate outdoor thermometer mounted somewhere near the yard. When the temperature reaches 80 degrees, a bulldog should not be left outdoors for more than five or ten minutes. To do otherwise is to court heatstroke.

Heatstroke, which occurs when rectal temperatures spike to 109.4°F (43°C) or when they linger around 106°F (41°C), destroys cell membranes and leads to organ failures. The dehydration that accompanies heatstrokes thickens the blood, which deprives tissues of necessary oxygen. The muscles, kidneys, liver, and gastrointestinal tract also may be affected. Moreover, heatstroke can cause swelling and subsequent damage to the brain, blindness, hemorrhages, convulsions, and fatal seizures.

If your bulldog becomes overheated and pants excessively after being outdoors, take his temperature at once. If his temperature is elevated, give him some cold water to drink and then reduce his temperature slowly with a cold-water bath. You should also have lemon juice on hand to squirt against the back of your bulldog's throat. This will cut through the accumulated mucus, thereby helping your dog to breath easier.

in houses or apartments without yards should be walked 10 or 15 minutes at least once a day (again, weather permitting)—this is in addition to their constitutional walks—and should be taken two or three times a week to an area where they can enjoy a little frolic under their owners' supervision.

Gifts often come with strings attached, and the bulldog's modest

Inherited Problems in Bulldogs
Hip Dysplasia: A malformation of the hip joint resulting in a poor fit between the head of the femur bone and the hip socket, in which the femoral head normally lies. Can be alleviated by surgery.

Luxating Patella: A dislocation of the patella, the small, flat, moveable bone at the front of the knee. In mild

Hip dysplasia, a degeneration of the socket in which the head of the femur bone rests, is one of several genetic diseases that can affect bulldogs.

cases the patella, which is held in place by ligaments, pops out of the groove in the femur in which it normally resides, then pops back in of its own accord. In severe cases the patella cannot return to its correct position on its own, and when it is manipulated into place, does not remain there long. A bulldog with luxating patella favors his affected leg when he walks, and when he runs, he lifts it, setting it down only every few steps.

The tendency toward luxating patella is inherited, but excess weight can aggravate that tendency. Luxating patella can be corrected by surgery.

Cherry eye: A swelling of a gland in the inner eyelid. This is a common condition in bulldogs and is usually treated by cutting the gland out if the swelling is a reoccurring problem.

Pigmentary keratitis: This condition is characterized by the deposition

"You talkin' to me? I don't see anybody else here. You must be talkin' to me."

"When coach said to let the air out of the ball, how was I to know he simply meant to play a little slower?"

Splendor in the grass: two bulldogs soaking up a little shade.

of pigment or melanin on the surface of the eye by the cornea in response to unrelieved irritation and/or inflammation. Pigmentary keratitis is nature's way of telling bulldog breeders they have gone too far in their quest for facial extremity. As breeders shortened the bulldog's muzzle, they also created the bulldog's excessive nasal folds and shallow eye sockets. The latter cause the eyes to protrude, and if they protrude overmuch, the eyelids cannot fully cover and protect the cornea, nor can they distribute the tear film effectively over the entire surface of the eye. This condition is known as lagophthalmos, and it is one of the causes of prolapsed eyes and of dry eye or keratoconjunctivitis (KCS). Other irritating factors include ingrown eyelashes (trichiasis), aberrant eyelid hairs (distichiasis), and trauma to the eye.

Pigmentary keratitis can be permanent if the cause of the irritation or inflammation is not removed—by surgery, if necessary—be it excessive nasal fold tissue, ingrown hairs, or KCS. After the cause of the problem has been eliminated, superficial deposits of pigment can be treated with topical eye medications. Pigment deep within the cornea may not be so easily treated, and if it impairs a bull-dog's vision, it should be removed surgically.

Elongated soft palate: This occurs in bulldogs and other short-faced breeds. It often results in some degree of obstruction of the dog's airway. This obstruction results in snorting, snoring, and breathing through the mouth. In severe cases of elongated palate, the palate partially blocks the opening into the voice box. If secondary changes in the voice box take place, acute airway obstruction may occur. If your bulldog begins to honk like a goose, put his head back, and gasp for air, consult your veterinarian to see if he or she considers your bulldog a candidate for the surgery necessary to correct an elongated soft palate.

It goes without saying, which is why it needs to be said, that sensible breeders will not use bulldogs suffering from pigmentary keratitis or any other inherited defect in their breeding programs. In bulldogs, as in all breeds, the dramatic is shadowed closely by the detrimental.

Because not all breeders are as conscientious as they should be, persons acquiring a bulldog should ask the seller who will be responsible for the vet bills if a bulldog should be victimized by an obviously inherited condition later in life.

Obedience Training

Despite the determined set of its jaw, the bulldog is not constitutionally opposed to training. In fact, the bulldog can be an apt and obliging pupil if you are an apt and obliging teacher. What you are obliged to be as a teacher is cheerful, patient, fair, firm, self-assured, attentive to your bulldog's behavior, and, if you wish, in possession of a pocketful of treats to advance your bully's education.

To Feed or Not to Feed

Until recently the use of food as a dog-training aid was about as welcome in training circles as a Hawaiian shirt at a black-tie affair. Indeed, even though food rewards are in vogue these days, there are still some trainers who refer to food sneeringly as a bribe, but treats make initial training much more interesting to your dog.

If you have designs on obedience competition, you will have to wean your dog away from immediate food rewards, which are not allowed in the show ring; and even if you do not intend to compete in obedience after you have taught your dog to sit, stay, come, and so on, you should gradually use food as an intermittent reward only. There may come a time when your bully is about to wander off into trouble, and you will want him to return to you even though you do not have a treat in your hand.

The Age of Consent

Basic training, which essentially consists of teaching your bulldog where he should conduct his personal affairs (see The Secret of House-Training, page 24), should begin as soon as you acquire him. As this training progresses, your bulldog will learn that certain behaviors are met with praise, and the satisfaction he gets from being praised is the foundation on which additional obedience training will be built.

Most bulldogs are ready to start obedience training of a more formal sort when they are six months old. Some may be ready a bit sooner; others may not be so soon. Your knowledge of your bulldog's mental capacity and maturity will help you to recognize when the time is right. Because larger breeds like the bulldog can be a challenge as they mature, especially if they possess the male bully's dominant spirit, you and your male bulldog might benefit from his participation in puppy kindergarten obedience classes if such are offered in your area.

Who's the Boss?

Dogs always have depended on the ability to function as members of a pack to survive. This dependence leads them to seek our approval. In the wild, dogs and their ancestors live in a pack dominated by the alpha member, or leader, of the pack. The alpha dog, contrary to popular misperception, is usually a female who functions as judge, jury, sheriff, exalted ruler, and high priestess of the pack.

The dog's hot-wired inclination to follow the leader allows you to assume the role of the alpha dog in your pack, whether yours is a two-member pack, a four-pack, or a six-pack. As the leader of the pack you have the right, among other things, to eat first, to sit, stand, or lie down wherever you want,

This bulldog's sweet expression belies his rough-and-ready heritage.

to go through a doorway first, to have your dog follow where you lead, to remove objects from your dog's mouth if you so desire, and to interrupt any activity that is harmful to your property

With a little coaxing, bulldogs will jump through hoops to please their owners.

or your dog's well-being. You also have the right not to be bitten, bothered when you are eating, bumped off course when you are walking, or bowled over by an exuberant dog.

Training Tips

1. Keep training sessions brief: 10 to 15 minutes at a time, once or twice a day, at least three times a week.

2. Conduct training sessions in the same location with the same unfailing patience each time. After your bulldog has mastered a command, you should vary the setting to see if he obeys in other locations as readily as he does at home.

3. Reward your bulldog with praise and, if you wish, treats when he does well. If he associates performance with good feelings, he will be more likely to perform willingly.

4. Do not use your bulldog's name to scold him if he makes a mistake during training. In fact, do not scold your bulldog at all during training. When he makes a mistake, show him what you want him to do, then praise him as if he had done it correctly.

5. Limit your bulldog to one teacher. Different folks have different strokes when handling dogs. This can play havoc with your dog's mind.

6. Do not let a training session end unless you are ready to end it. If your bulldog attempts to retire before a training session is over, bring him back quietly and try again. Do not call him by name when you are trying to coax him back to the training site.

7. If you are practicing in the house, have a lead handy in case the doorbell rings and you have to answer it. Put the lead on your bulldog and walk him to the door. Send the person away and go back to your training session. Of course you will not have to bother answering the phone during a training session. That is why answering machines were invented.

8. Let other members of the household know that you do not wish to be disturbed during a training session.

9. If your bulldog is not catching on to a lesson as quickly as you would like, ask yourself what you are doing wrong. Have you defined the behavior in a way the dog can understand? Are you going too quickly? Are you handling your bulldog too abruptly? Has an impatient tone infiltrated your voice? Are you rewarding your bulldog as soon as he does the right thing? Is it time to take a step back and go over a routine he already knows for a few days in order to build up his confidence before coming back to the behavior that is giving him trouble?

10. Never repeat a command. If you tell your dog to sit and he does not, put him in a sitting position, step back, and praise him. If you keep repeating "sit" until he does, you will be teaching him that the first "sit" (or the first ten "sits") does not count.

What's in a Name?

Quite often a dog's name (and a feeling of confusion) are the only things he brings to his new home. If your bulldog has a name and knows what it is, why not use that name? You may shorten it some, if possible, or reshape it to something less hideous, but your bulldog will have enough to do adjusting to a new home without having to adjust to a new identity as well.

If your bulldog has not been named by his breeder or if he has not yet learned his name, you can teach him to respond to whatever name you choose by rewarding him with extravagant praise every time he does. Suppose you have decided to name your bulldog Butch. While you are playing with him or sitting quietly with him, pronounce his name with a high-pitched, ascending gusto on the first syllable. If he looks in any direction

"All I have to do is jump over this big log."

but yours, do nothing. Wait a second or two and say his name again. Unless he is stone deaf, Butch will look toward you eventually. When he

Although bulldogs once lived to fight, now they are lovers, not fighters.

61

There is nothing sweeter than the sound of a dog's name, especially when spoken by a person with a treat in his hand.

nose. As soon as he shows any interest in the treat, move your treat hand back past his eyes toward the top of his head. As your hand moves, Butch will more than likely raise his head to follow the progress of the treat; and, in a perfect world, he will sit down naturally as a result of raising his head. Right before his butt touches the ground, say "sit" once and reward him with the treat after he touches down.

If Butch backs away from you in order to get a better look at the treat, take a step or two away from him, show him the treat and repeat the exercise. Be careful not to say "sit" again until right before he has done so.

If Butch still does not sit, you will have to show him what you want him to do. Take his collar in one hand and, as you are pulling up on the collar, say "sit" and push down on his rump with your other hand until he assumes the sitting position. Give him the treat, and after he has been sitting pretty for a few seconds, say "Okay" to let him know that it is all right for him to stand up.

does, say "good" and reward him with a jackpot of hugs, pets, and kisses and, if you want, a treat.

So now you have Butch's attention. Wait a minute or two until he turns his attention elsewhere, then say his name once more. You may have to say it twice or even three times, but if you put enough excitement into your tone, Butch will look at you again. When he does, make a fuss over him as you did before, and give him a treat.

After Butch has responded to his name three or four times in one session, you have accomplished your mission. If you repeat that mission two or three times a day for a week, you will have Butch's attention any time you call his name, and he will come to realize that the sound of his name has a special meaning all his own.

Once Butch begins to respond regularly to "sit" or to any other command, do not give him a food reward every time he obeys properly. If he knows he can get a treat every time, he may decide on occasion that it is more rewarding to continue what he was doing, even if he was doing nothing, than to get that old predictable treat. But if he does not get a treat every time, he will not be certain that treats are always forthcoming. Thus, he will be more likely to obey every time because he always will be hoping that this time is the charm.

A Quartet of Useful Commands

Sit

This is the easiest lesson to teach, so you should teach it first. Simply stand facing Butch and hold a treat in your right hand at the level of his

Psychologists call this maybe-yes, maybe-no technique *positive intermittent reinforcement*. They caution, however, that the schedule of intermittent reinforcement must not be predictable. If you withhold the treat every third time you give Butch a command, he will soon begin timing his refusals to coincide with the empty hand. To be effective, intermittent reinforcement must be random. If your training sessions consist of four or five practices of a command during two or three sessions a day, withhold the treat the second time you give Butch that command during the first session, the fourth time during the second session, and so on.

Do not be intermittent with your praise, however. You do not want Butch thinking that you love him less for some performances than for others. Every time he obeys a command, say "good boy," even if you do not give him a treat.

When Butch has mastered the sit routine, you can teach him to sit while he is walking on lead. Begin by walking him on your left side with the lead in your left hand as usual, then come to a halt. When you do, switch the lead to your right hand and say "sit." If he sits, great. If he hesitates, position your right hand above his head, pull up lightly on the lead, and, at the same time, place your left hand on his rump and press down gently. Once Butch sits down, praise him quietly, but control your enthusiasm. You want him to remain sitting. If he stands up, repeat the sit command. After Butch has been sitting for a few seconds, say "Butch, heel" and continue walking. After several paces, repeat the "sit" command. Do this another two or three times and end the lesson.

As you repeat the sit command on subsequent days, Butch should need less and less prompting from the pull of his collar on his neck and the push of your hand on his rump. He has mastered the sit command when he can come to a stop and sit promptly when he hears the word sit while walking on a lead. Eventually whenever you come to a halt, he will stop and sit without having to be told.

Stay

After Butch has mastered the sit command, you can begin teaching him to stay. With Butch in the sitting position on your left and the lead in your left hand, lean down and place your right hand—palm toward your dog—about 6 inches (15 cm) in front of his face. Say "stay" and after you do, move slowly around until you are standing directly in front of Butch and your right hand is held in front of his face as though you were a police officer stopping traffic. The lead still will be in your left hand at this point, so if Butch begins to move toward you, pull the lead straight up gently to keep him in place.

After Butch has stayed in position for five seconds or so, release him by saying "Okay." Praise him and give him a treat if you wish. Then take up the lead with Butch at your left, walk several paces, tell him to sit, and after he does, repeat the stay command. Practice this command three or four more times before you end the lesson. As you practice the stay command on subsequent days, slowly increase the amount of time Butch stays in place before you release him.

When Butch has mastered the stay command, you can begin to increase the distance between you and him while he is staying in place. Give him the stay command, set the lead on the ground, and take a small step or two away from him. Repeat the stay command, with the raised-hand signal for reinforcement, if Butch looks as if he is about to move. Return him to the sitting position if he does move. After he has stayed in place for ten or 15 seconds, release him and praise him for being a good dog.

During the course of several training sessions gradually increase the distance between you and Butch to ten yards (9.1 m). Then, instead of giving the stay command and backing away

A practical application of the "sit" command.

Bulldogs have two "best" sides: the left, shown here, and the right.

from him, give the command and, leading off with your right foot, walk ten or 12 paces, then turn and face him. If he has learned his lessons well, he ought to be sitting obediently in place. If he has followed you instead, take him back to his original position and repeat the exercise; but this time after giving the stay command, walk only one or two steps before turning and facing him.

Come

After you have taught Butch to sit and to stay, teaching him to come should not be difficult. First tell Butch to sit, then walk five or six paces away from him, turn, and face him. Taking a treat out of your pocket, hold out the treat and say, "come." If you put enough gusto into your voice, Butch will come bounding over to get the treat. At that point, you can praise him and give him the treat, or you can ask him to sit before praising and giving him the treat.

If, for some reason, Butch remains sitting or goes wandering off to do something else when you call him to come, put a lead on him, tell him to sit, and repeat the command. If he ignores you this time, give the lead short, authoritative tugs, and reel him in to the place where you are standing. Do not repeat "come," and do not not give him the treat, but do praise him as if he had obeyed you.

Praising a dog that has just ignored you might seem unwise, but you would be even less wise to allow Butch to ignore you when he pleases. By moving Butch to the place where you want him to be, you are teaching him that he is either going to come when he is called or you are going to see that he does. By praising him you are showing him that there are no hard feelings even if he did misunderstand you.

Leave the lead on Butch, tell him to sit, walk to the end of the lead, and ask him to come again. After Butch has complied with the "come" command two or three times—willingly or by your reeling him in—end the lesson. In this as in all other lessons, never end on a disobedient note. The last request you make of your dog should be obeyed, even if you have to fake obedience by walking him through the command.

Eventually, Butch should begin responding to the "come" command with little more than a gentle tug on the lead by way of spiritual guidance. This is your signal to eliminate the tug after you have called him. If he responds to your voice only, his reward should be generous. If he is not yet voice activated, revert to tugging on the lead as a means of inspiring him to come when called.

When that glorious day on which Butch comes to you in response to your voice alone finally dawns, bask in the glory of several more of those days. Then try the exercise without the benefit of the lead. If Butch ignores you, go back to the lead.

Repeat the come exercise two or three times a day, limiting the distance Butch has to travel to 4 or 5 feet and restricting each session to two or three minutes in which Butch has answered your call three or four times. After Butch is coming to you consistently when you call, increase the distance between you and him by gradual increments: first, to 6 or 7 feet for several days and then to 8 or 9 feet for the next several days. Keep increasing the distance between you and him until he responds to your command from across the yard or across a room.

Initially, there are only two reasons that a bulldog can see for coming when he is called: praise and food. (Eventually, force of habit will be added to this short list.) Therefore, when you are training Butch to come

when he is called, he expects you to be happy that he responded. Never call him when you want to give him medication, scold him, or do anything else that might cause him discomfort. If he associates a summons with an unpleasant consequence, he will begin ignoring all summonses.

After Butch has learned to come faithfully when you call, you can reduce the lavish praise to a simple "good boy" or a pat on the head by way of intermittent reinforcement. Do not eliminate the reinforcement altogether or you risk eliminating his willing response.

Down

The down command is taught with the lead on. Begin by placing Butch at your left in the sit position. Stoop, bend, crouch, or kneel alongside him—whichever is most comfortable—and hold a treat in front of his nose. As soon as he shows interest in the treat, move it very slowly down and away from him in an arcing L shape. As you do, say "down."

Unless Butch is seriously ill, he will lunge for the treat. If he stands up when he does, withdraw the treat, put him in the sit position once again, and

A bulldog being shown the meaning of "down."

repeat the exercise. This time lean your left arm across his back to keep him from rising and to inspire him to stretch his front feet forward into the down position as he lunges for the treat. If he stands up or does anything but assume the down position, withdraw the treat, put him in the sit position, and try again. You may have to try this exercise several times before you finally get Butch where you want him. After you do, be sure to praise him and to give him the treat. Make sure that he consumes the treat in the down position, then release him and praise him again.

Not the Last Word

This chapter is the first word, not the last, on dog training. You can certainly get a leg up by studying this chapter, but beyond that you should also take your dog to obedience class.

The interaction with other dogs and their owners will do both of you good, and that interaction is most important for dogs that are the only canine members of their packs.

One of the best bits of training advice ever written is the suggestion that we eliminate the word "no" from our training vocabularies. Whenever your dog makes a mistake, instead of saying no, simply show him what you want him to do, then praise him for having done it. (If you must express verbal exasperation, say *aaaaaaahhhhh* in a mild, neutral-to-slightly-disappointed tone.) You and your dog will make better progress if you inspire him with success rather than mold him with correction. Think of training as a multiple-choice test: The right answer is in there someplace, you just have to help your dog to find it.

The Show Must Go On

If ever you are seized by the inspiration to show your bulldog, ask yourself why. Unless you are the rare sort of person whose house was the only one on the block not julienned when the tornado came to town, you will lose more often than you will win. In the process you may develop neuroses for which you did not even know you were harboring the potential. You will, furthermore, find yourself becoming superstitious, crabby at home, aggressive in traffic, shopping for new clothes you do not really need, and unable to concentrate on work or other mundane affairs several days before and after a show. Moreover, the numbers on your odometer will wax while those in your checking account will wane. If you choose to continue reading, therefore, we must ask to be absolved from any changes to your personality or marital status that arise from showing your dog.

Buying a Show Dog

Persons who have the inclination to get involved in showing their bulldogs should make that desire clear to the breeder when they go to look at puppies. Many first-time dog owners could not have cared less about showing when they brought their pups home, but after being told several times at the park or the feed store that they "ought to show that dog," they convince themselves that a dog is a show prospect simply because he has a pedigree. Pedigrees do not show dogs make, however. Indeed, most pedigreed dogs are not show quality, even if you define *show quality* as "good

enough to earn a championship." (If the truth be known, most dogs can "earn" championships if they live long enough and get dragged to enough shows by the right handler.)

If you are suddenly overcome by a desire to show the bulldog you purchased at a pet price, consult the dog's breeder first. Breeders are not opposed to ugly ducklings that have turned into swans being shown, but they are less than thrilled when less than perfect examples of their breeding programs turn up in the show ring accompanied by an overenthusiastic novice exhibitor. So before you begin to write to show superintendents for premium lists, ask the dog's breeder if you can take the dog around for an evaluation. If you bought your dog from a breeder who lives far away, ask a local breeder to evaluate your dog. An ounce of prevention can be worth a pound of disappointment in the show ring.

Anyone interested in showing and eventually breeding bulldogs should start with the best quality female possible—preferably one from a well-established kennel with an impressive show record. Novices are at an even greater disadvantage evaluating talent in a dog than they are when gauging his personality and general state of health. A runny eye is a runny eye to most observers, but eyes of the proper size, shape, and setting are more difficult for newcomers to identify. Before you buy a show dog, visit dog shows, talk to bulldog breeders, watch bulldog classes being judged, and learn what winning bulldogs look

More than just a pretty face, this bulldog is an athlete, too.

like. If possible, visit several bulldog breeders who are willing to spend some time explaining what to look for in a show dog.

Most important, study the bulldog breed standard. Take a copy of the standard and, if the breeder does not object, another breeder with you when you go to look at puppies. Ask the seller to point out where a puppy or a dog meets the standard and where he does not. And bear in mind that being pick of the litter is no guarantee that a

The light at the end of this tunnel is a bulldog.

puppy will be a judge's pick in the show ring.

Because breeders with the best available puppies will not always live within driving distance, you may have nothing more on which to base an informed decision than a few pictures and the breeder's evaluation. If the pictures are unclear, ask to see more. If you have any reason to doubt the breeder's word, find another breeder. In any case, ask the breeder to say, preferably in writing, where a puppy measures up to the standard and where he falls short.

Anyone buying a show dog also is buying the genes that dog has inherited from his ancestors. The names and titles of the first four or five generations of ancestors are recorded on a dog's pedigree. Review the pedigree carefully to see how many members of a puppy's family are champions. The more champions present in a puppy's pedigree, the better his ancestors have done in competition, and the better his chances, on paper at least, of carrying on the family tradition.

When looking at a pedigree, look most closely at the first two generations. A puppy inherits 50 percent of his genetic makeup from each of his parents, 25 percent from any grandparent, and 12.5 percent from any great-grandparent. Each dog in the fourth generation contributes 6.25 percent to a puppy's genetic makeup. Obviously, dogs that far removed from the present are not going to make much of a splash in a puppy's gene pool.

Although some puppies never look anything but promising from an early age, the average youngster goes through several stages while growing up. Today's swan can be tomorrow's ugly duckling. He may be a swan again the day after tomorrow, but how are you to know? That is why you should wait until a potential show-quality puppy has gone through the duckling phase before you sign any checks. The puppy's breeder should be familiar enough with his or her dogs to know when they are old enough to make a reliable final decision—as reliable as these sorts of decisions ever are.

Where the Shows Are

The American Kennel Club (AKC) recognizes more than 140 breeds of dogs and sanctions roughly 10,000 competitive events each year. These gatherings include conformation shows, obedience trials, and field trials. Many AKC events are advertised in dog magazines. If you simply want to attend a show, buy one of these magazines at a newsstand, supermarket, or feed store. If you cannot find a dog magazine with a list of shows in it, call one of the magazines' subscription departments (see Useful Groups and Addresses, page 90) and ask to buy the latest issue. Newspapers may also contain listings for local shows in the "Pets" section of the classified ads or in the notices of coming events in the "Living," "Lifestyle," or "Weekend" sections.

If you are interested in entering your bulldog in a show, you will need the names and addresses of the superintendents who manage shows. These are the persons from whom you can obtain premium lists for the shows you want to enter. A list of superintendents is printed each month in *Dog World* magazine and in the *Events Calendar*, published by the AKC.

The Premium List and Entry Form

A premium list contains information about a scheduled show and the entry form you need to enter a dog in that show. Premium lists provide the date and location of the show, the names of the judges for each breed eligible to compete in the show, directions to the

Bulldog owners can read about their favorite breed in two bulldog publications (see page 90).

show site, information about overnight camping facilities, the date on which entry forms are due at the superintendent's office, and lists of special prizes offered at the show.

Premium lists are available from show superintendents. To obtain premium lists for shows in your area, write to one or two superintendents and ask to be put on their mailing lists. If there is a specific show for which you want to obtain a premium list, include that request in your letter.

Once an entry form is completed, mail it with the appropriate fee (or fax it, along with a credit card number) to the show superintendent. Entries generally cost between $16 and $20 (a little less at some shows for puppy or bred-by-exhibitor classes), and they are usually due at the superintendent's office 18 days or so before the day of a show.

About one week before the show, you will receive a confirmation packet from the superintendent. It will contain an entry slip, a judging schedule, the number of entries for each breed, and the numbers of the rings in which the various breeds will be judged.

A dog show is a fascinating combination of beauty pageant and social event.

The entry confirmation also contains a facsimile of your dog's listing in the show catalog. Check this listing carefully to make sure all names are spelled correctly, your dog's registration number is accurate, and your dog has been entered in the correct class. If you find any errors, report them to the superintendent as soon as you reach the show site. You may have to ask two or three people where the superintendent is located, but he or she will not be difficult to find.

Varieties of Competition

As a novice exhibitor you will more than likely be interested in conformation shows or obedience trials. In the former, which are open to unaltered dogs only, entries are judged on appearance and movement. In obedience trials, in which neutered males and spayed bitches may also compete, dogs are judged on their ability to obey specific commands.

Types of Shows

Whether you choose to enter a conformation or an obedience show, you have three types of events from which

to choose: the match show, the all-breed show, and the specialty show. The latter two shows (all-breed and specialty) are also known as point shows because dogs and bitches competing in them may win points toward championship or obedience titles.

Match Shows

Match shows offer inexperienced exhibitors and/or their dogs a chance to learn their way around the ring in a relaxed setting. Although match shows are similar to point shows, no points toward championships or other titles are awarded at match shows, nor do match-show judges have to be licensed by the AKC. What's more, puppies as young as three months of age may be entered in a match show. (At point shows puppies must be at least six months old in order to compete.)

All-breed Shows

These are AKC-licensed shows at which all 140-plus breeds recognized for championship competition are eligible to compete for points toward their championship or obedience titles. Entries at all-breed shows regularly exceed 1,000, and shows with 2,000 or even more are not uncommon.

Specialty Shows

These are AKC-licensed shows in which only one breed is eligible to compete for championship points and other awards. The Bulldog Dog Club of America holds a national specialty show each September. In addition, regional bulldog clubs hold their own specialty shows throughout the year.

Group Shows

The AKC assigns each breed it recognizes to one of seven groups. Bulldogs belong to the nonsporting group. Occasionally a specialty show will be held with entries limited to dogs of a certain group. This kind of show is known as a group show.

Which Class to Enter

The majority of bulldogs compete in conformation shows. Thus, we will confine the present discussion to the mechanics and procedures relative to that kind of competition.

Winners in the different classes offered at conformation shows are nominally selected because they most closely approximate the kind of dog described in the written standard for the breed. In reality, breed standards are constructed broadly enough to allow men and women of goodwill to interpret them differently. As a result, a dog that was best in show on Friday might not even be best in its breed at the following day's show. Indeed, one dog-show judge has written that the continuing success of the dog fancy is based to an extent on inconsistent judging. Otherwise, the same dogs would win all the time and few people would bother to enter their dogs in shows.

In conformation shows, males (which are called *dogs*) and females (which are called *bitches*) are competing for points that will make them champions. They are also competing for best-of-breed, best-in-group, and best-in-show awards.

A dog or a bitch must earn 15 points to become a champion. Those points can be earned one, two, three, four, or five at a time, depending on the number of other entries a dog or a bitch defeats in competition. Before explaining what distinguishes a one- from a two- from a five-point win, we should describe the kinds of classes offered at all-breed and specialty shows.

All dogs and bitches that have not earned their championships compete against other nonchampion members of their breed and sex for points toward the championship title. Non-champion dogs or bitches, known as class dogs or class bitches respectively, may be entered in the first five classes described below. The breeder from whom you acquired your dog should be able to offer you guidance in deciding which class to enter.

The puppy class is for entries between six months and one day under 12 months of age. The puppy class is sometimes divided into a puppy six-to-nine-month class and a puppy nine-to-twelve-month class. In addition, classes for dogs and bitches 12 to 18 months old are offered at specialty shows and at some all-breed shows.

The novice class is for entries above one year of age that have never earned a first-place ribbon in another adult class. After a dog or bitch has earned three first-place ribbons in the novice class, it must be entered in one of the other adult classes at subsequent shows.

The bred-by-exhibitor class is for entries more than six months of age that are being shown by persons who bred and currently own them.

The American-bred class is for entries six months of age and older that were bred in the United States.

The open class is for any entry more than six months of age.

The winners class is for the winners of each of the five classes described above. This class is held immediately after the preceding five classes have been judged. You cannot enter this class in advance, you must win your way into it the day of the show.

The Mechanics of Judging

Nonchampion (or class) dogs usually are judged before nonchampion (or class) bitches. In each class the judge awards first- through fourth-place ribbons if the size and quality of the class warrant them. After all

A bulldog promenading in the show ring.

competes in the nonsporting group. The other groups are sporting, hound, working, terrier, toy, and herding.

Judges award first- through fourth-place ribbons in group competition. Lastly, the seven group winners compete for best in show at the end of the day.

Counting Up the Points

The number of points earned by the winners dog and the winners bitch are determined by the number of other class entries those winners defeat. This number, which is based upon the cumulative entries in a breed during the preceding show season, may vary from one region of the country to another, from one year to another, and from one breed to the next. For example, during the 1996 show season in Division 2 of the AKC, a division that comprises Delaware, New Jersey, Pennsylvania, and Ohio, two class (or nonchampion) bulldog dogs present and competing constituted a one-point show. Eight class dogs present and competing constituted a two-point show. Fifteen dogs constituted a three-point show; 23 dogs a four-point show; and 38 or more a five-point show. In bitches, two entries were required for a one-point show; eight for a two-point show; 15 for a three-point show; 23 for a four-point show; and 38 or more for a five-point show. No dog or bitch can earn more than five points at a time toward a championship, no matter how many entries are defeated.

All 15 points needed to become a conformation champion may not be accumulated one or two at a time, however. Two wins must be major wins, that is, wins that are worth three, four, or five points. And those major wins must come from two different judges.

Mathematically, the fastest a dog or a bitch can finish a championship is in

classes have been judged, winning dogs from the various classes return to the ring immediately for the winners class. The winner of that class—that is, the winners dog—receives points toward the champion title.

Class bitches are judged in the same class sequence as class dogs. Immediately after winners bitch has been chosen, the best-of-breed class is held. This class is for champions (also known as "specials") of both sexes and for winners dog and winners bitch at that day's show. In the best-of-breed class, all dogs and bitches compete for best of breed and best of opposite sex. In addition, the winners dog and the winners bitch compete for the best-of-winners ribbon.

At specialty shows the competition is over at this point. In all-breed shows best-of-breed winners return later in the day to compete in their respective groups. The best-of-breed bulldog three shows. In actuality it takes more shows than that. A lot more for the majority of champions. If you figure that it will take a bulldog an average of 15 to 20 shows to earn its championship, chances are you will be right more often than not.

Ring Procedure

Upon entering the ring, exhibitors line up their dogs or bitches down one side of the ring or, if the class is large, down two or more sides. Exhibitors then stack their dogs (see Stacking, page 74) while the judge walks down the line taking a first-impression look at each entry in the class.

The judge then asks the exhibitors to walk their dogs around the ring in a circle en masse. After the exhibitors come to a halt, the judge inspects each entry closely. After the judge has examined an entry, he or she asks the exhibitor to gait (or walk) the dog in one or two patterns (see Gaiting Patterns). Finally, after the judge has inspected every entry in a class, he or she may ask a few individuals to gait their entries again. At that point the judge may shuffle the order in which dogs are standing in the ring before asking the entire class to circle the ring again. The judge will then point to the first-, second-, third-, and fourth-place finishers in the class. These dogs and their exhibitors line up to receive their ribbons while the rest of the class leaves the ring. (In best-of-breed classes, the judge will indicate a maximum of three winners: best of breed, best of opposite sex, and best of winners.)

Practicing at Home

For practical reasons you should teach your bulldog to walk on a lead (see Lead Training, page 22), but you will need to refine that talent for the show ring. In the ring your bully should be willing to walk smartly at your left side, neither lagging behind nor surging ahead.

Gaiting Patterns

Exhibitors usually are asked to gait their dogs or bitches in one or more of three patterns: the circle, the down-and-back, and the triangle. To practice these patterns at home, all you need are your dog, a lead, a 40-by-50-foot (12.2 by 15.2 m) swatch of yard, and a pocketful of small treats.

The secret of showing—for you and your dog—is having a good time. Always begin each practice session with a minute or two of spirited petting and a few treats. You want your bully to react gleefully at the sight of a lead because she knows there are treats in store and a chance to be the center of attention.

In the down-and-back pattern, your bulldog walks on your left for 15 or 20 feet (4.5 or 6.1 m), makes a right U-turn smartly, then walks back to the starting spot. As you bring your bully to a halt, hold a treat a few feet in front of her face, slightly above eye level, to get her attention. Bulldogs are supposed to look attentive, but if your dog starts to rise up on her hind legs,

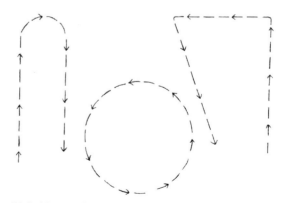

Walk this way: Bulldogs and exhibitors are expected to step smartly through these patterns in the show ring.

say "no" or "down." Do not give her the treat until she has all four feet on the ground and is standing still for five or ten seconds.

Because dogs are not supposed to sit in the show ring, do not allow your bulldog to sit down while you are practicing. If she does, just say "no" and snap the lead briefly until she stands up.

In the circle pattern you keep your bulldog on your left while walking a circle with an eight- to ten-foot (2.43 to 3.01 m) radius. At the end of each circle bring your bulldog to a halt, show her the treat, and after she is standing still five to ten seconds, reward her with praise and the treat.

Stacking is the art of positioning a dog to accentuate her good qualities while minimizing her deficiencies.

In the triangle pattern you walk 10 to 20 feet (4.5 to 6.1 m), turn left, walk another 10 to 15 feet (3.01 to 4.5 m), then return to the starting point on the diagonal. Repeat the exhibitor-shows-treat, dog-poses-handsomely routine at the end.

You do not have to practice these patterns more than ten minutes or so every second or third day. After that, practice only as much as you and your dog need to in order to remain crisp.

In addition to teaching a bulldog good ring manners, lead training should develop the gaiting speed at which a bulldog looks most natural. In short, you and your bulldog should look relaxed in the ring. Practice walking in an easy, yet purposeful manner, keeping one eye on the dog and the other on the judge. Do not allow your bulldog to sniff the ground or to walk with her head drooping. If your bulldog begins sniffing or ducking her head, a short tug on the lead will bring her head to the desired position. Do not jerk the lead strongly. The idea is to get your dog's attention, not to lift her off her feet. The lead is a corrective, not a coercive, device.

Stacking

Stacking is the art of positioning a dog so as to accentuate her best qualities and to minimize her flaws. With the lead on your dog, position her so that she is standing with her front legs foursquare. If necessary, get down on one or both knees and set your bully's legs in place. If your bulldog tends to toe one front leg in or out, turn that leg to the desired position (always turn from the top, not the middle, of the leg) and set that leg in place first. Position the hind legs in the same manner. When your bulldog is looking camera-ready, hold a treat in your right hand a few feet in front of her face, slightly above nose level, so that she will hold that pose for at least a minute.

Do You Need a Handler?

Showing a bulldog does not require as much fleetness of foot or deftness of comb as showing some other breeds demands. A reasonably coordinated and self-confident person should be able to show his or her own dog. If you prefer, however, you can hire the services of a professional dog handler. A professional handler knows tricks that a novice could be a long time learning, and a professional is known by more judges than a novice is. Handlers charge $50 to $75 to show a dog, and if they have to take your dog with them overnight, you will subsidize a portion of their traveling, lodging, and eating expenses, too.

Provisions for a Show

The most important items to pack for a show are the entry slip and show confirmation, the lead, some treats, a folding chair, and a spray bottle filled with water. (You will need the latter if your bulldog gets overheated.)

The incidental items packed for a show are determined by personal comfort. Some exhibitors pack enough

Basic Show Supplies Checklist

flea comb.....................................☐
brush ....☐
cotton swabs ....☐
cotton balls..................................☐
paper towels................................☐
facial tissues...............................☐
washcloth ....☐
eye drops ....☐
pen ....☐
can opener ....☐
bottle opener ....☐
first-aid kit...................................☐
food ....☐
spoon ....☐
biodegradable paper plates ....☐
bottled water from home ....☐
water bowl....................................☐
magazine or book ....☐
pooper scooper ....☐
small plastic baggies....................☐

provisions for a two-month stay in a biosphere. Others pack more conservatively. The above checklist therefore, is intended merely as a guide.

Should You Breed Your Bulldog?

Dog breeders are fond of talking about "improving the breed." And why not? This sounds like a noble mission. What's more, it rolls impressively off the tongue, marking the speaker as a person of serious mien and lofty intent, especially if the speaker delivers the phrase with head tilted ever so slightly skyward and eyes fixed on the horizon, as if envisioning a goal beyond the ken of mere mortals to envision.

The Facts About Breeding

What would bulldogs think about this business of improving the breed? Since bullies are the ones breeders are working so diligently to improve, should not someone stop to ask how, precisely, bulldogs might want to be improved? One suspects they might

Do not try this at home. A puppy does not make a good Christmas present.

like to do their own breeding, something very few bulldogs accomplish without humans getting involved during the process. Bullies might also like to be able to go for a decent walk on a warm day without risking heat prostration. They might like to be able to deliver their young without the imposition of a C-section. They might further wish they did not get cherry eye, suffer from sleep apnea, and play host to a variety of skin disorders. Any decent breeding program should be designed with these goals in mind at least, wouldn't you think?

What Are Your Plans?

In real life the ability to improve the breed is way beyond the scope of most breeders. The best that most people can hope to do is to leave the breed no worse than they found it after they decide to get their dogs neutered or spayed and move on to another hobby. Therefore, if you want to breed bulldogs, you should know in advance how you plan to avoid contributing to the problems that beset this breed. This means you have to study—and study intently—the histories of the dogs with which you plan to work. You must learn their weaknesses as well as their strengths, and never breed to obtain the latter at the expense of contributing to the former. Your first responsibility as a breeder is to your puppies' good health—not to the standard, nor to the show ring, and particularly not to the notions of fame, glory, or money.

At a time when nearly three million purebred puppies are born each year and one quarter of the dogs destroyed in animal shelters for lack of good homes are purebred, the decision to bring more puppies into the world is not one to be made lightly. For most people it is not one that should be made or even contemplated at all.

If you are not certain you will make your puppies as happy as they make you—and that you can find homes for them that are as good as the one you will provide while they are in your care—then you should not set about making puppies at all. In fact, you never should produce a litter for which you do not have good homes already—or the unwavering intention of providing a good home, namely yours, for any puppy you cannot place. And do not include on your list of qualified, prospective owners any family member or friend who says casually that he or she would love to have a puppy. Those are not promises, they are wishes; and wishes generally evaporate a few minutes after you ring someone up and say, "I've got that puppy you were looking for."

One hopes that most readers have skipped to another section of the book by now. If you are trudging purposefully onward at this point, perhaps you are merely curious, or perhaps you are the rare individual who is responsible enough to be entrusted with the privilege of raising puppies. If so, there are two more things you need to understand: much can go wrong in a planned mating, and in the animal world anything that can go wrong generally will sooner or later.

The Female's Heat Cycle

A heat cycle or season, also known as *estrus*, is a period of sexual receptivity that occurs in most mammalian females, dogs included. Estrus (from the Greek word for "mad passion") first

"You may take my picture now."

occurs between 10 and 14 months of age in the majority of female dogs. Male dogs, for their part, are always in season. They generally become sexually mature at about the same time females do.

You can be fairly certain that your female is in season if she begins to

Bulldog mothers should be supervised at feeding time.

emit a dark, bloody vaginal discharge and to exhibit vulvar swelling. Just as you are noticing bloodstains on your floors and carpets, unaltered male dogs in your neighborhood will notice the scent of pheromones, chemical substances discharged from your bulldog bitch's vulva and excreted in her urine. To be certain no unexpected matings take place, never leave your soon-to-be-willing bitch in the yard by herself after she has come into season, no matter how sturdy you think your fence is. Mating is the mother of invention, and unlike most bulldog studs, dogs of other breeds or of mixed-breed ancestry may well be able to breed your bully without your assistance.

Females do not ovulate as soon as they come into season; nor are they usually willing to accept a male's advances at that juncture. For the first six to nine days or so that they are in season—a period technically known as *proestrus*—females will be uncooperative or aggressive if a male attempts copulation.

When her vaginal discharge changes color from dark red to pinkish or watermelon red, a bitch goes into a *standing heat* or true estrus, the second phase of the heat cycle. If she is approached by a male during this phase of her cycle, which generally lasts six to twelve days, she will raise her tail, flag it to one side, lift her pelvis, and present her vulva.

When to Breed

Ovulation, the release of eggs from the ovaries, usually occurs some time during a female's standing heat, although it can occur in middle to late proestrus. Once the eggs are released, they must mature roughly 72 hours before they are ready to be fertilized. After that they have only 48 to 72 hours to live. Fortunately, sperm can survive inside a female for up to seven days. Even more fortunately, blood tests can determine the optimum time for breeding a female. Your veterinarian should be able to tell you if there are reproductive specialists in your area who can administer these tests. If there are no such vets in your vicinity, perhaps your veterinarian can draw blood from your female and send it off to be analyzed, or perhaps your veterinarian will be able to tell from examining a vaginal smear when your female is ready to be bred. If all else fails, you can breed your bulldog bitch on the 10th, 12th, and 14th days from the first time you noticed she was in heat. Be sure to count the day you first make this discovery as day one.

Breed the Best to the Best

The Female

Only healthy, well-adjusted females that have been in season at least once, are 18 months old, and are descended from dogs free of major genetic defects should be considered for breeding. Among bulldogs, the bitch descended from the rare free-whelping mother (i.e., one who can deliver puppies on her own) is an especially prime candidate for breeding.

The Male

In searching for a stud dog, you should have three items on your shopping list: the stud should live in a surgically clean household; he should come from a family or a line of dogs that has produced nice puppies when bred to your female's line in the past; and he should have proven himself capable of producing those qualities your bitch lacks. If your bitch could use heavier bone, for example, there is little chance of her producing heavy-boned puppies if the male you are considering has produced only medium-boned pups as a rule.

Genetics is so unpredictable that only the most carefully planned breedings have better than a crapshoot chance of producing quality bulldogs. In fact, the best a breeder can do in any breeding (ad)venture is to minimize the chances for failure. For this reason you should consider using an older stud dog, one who is already a grandfather, because it is easier to judge a male's reproductive potential by looking at his children and their children than by looking at the ribbons he has won. Too many people scurry off to breed to the latest winner, who may have proven himself in the show ring but who has yet to prove himself otherwise—and whose success may be more a function of style or politics than substance. This year's glamour bulldogs may develop into top producers one day, but for now it is more demonstrable that their fathers and mothers already have.

Contracts and Paperwork

Although they have little direct control over a dog's genes, breeders can legislate the mating process. Do not breed your bulldog to any male whose owner is not willing to provide a current health certificate for that dog. Be wary of sending your female to breeders who do not ask you to supply the same document.

The stud-service contract is another document that should accompany all breeding arrangements. Such a contract—like all contracts—becomes a legally binding document once it has been freely signed by two parties of sufficient age and mental capacity. Oral agreements are also legally binding, but, (by definition) cannot be documented so easily.

The stud-service contract does not have to be complicated or lengthy, but it should declare the fee involved and, if applicable, the responsibilities of the stud owner while the female is in his or her care, the length of time the stud owner is willing to keep the female, and the boarding fee, if any, that the stud owner charges for feeding and housing visiting females. The stud-service contract also should stipulate what happens if the female is mated but does not conceive; if she conceives but loses her puppies prematurely after she returns home; if she has only one live puppy; and any other eventuality that the parties to the contract consider important enough to put in writing.

Raising Puppies

The first outward sign that a bitch is pregnant is a modest swelling about the nipples. This enlargement, accompanied by a change in skin tone from flesh pink to rosy pink, occurs four to five weeks after conception. By then, each puppy embryo a bitch is carrying is little more than the size of a walnut (15 to 30 mm). Toward the end of the eighth week of pregnancy, the fetal skeleton is visible on abdominal radiographs. Many bulldog owners have their bitches x-rayed at this point to get an idea of how many puppies they are carrying. The terms *natural delivery* and *bulldog bitch* are, for all intents and purposes, mutually exclusive because of the bulldog's large head and other structural anomalies. Therefore, you should have scheduled your bitch's C-section by the time of her predelivery exam.

There is always one puppy looking for a good time long after the others are ready for a nap.

Care During Pregnancy

Some bulldog owners interpret the changing colors on their bitches' underbellies as a call to action. They start adding vitamins and minerals to their bitches' meals, and those meals begin to grow faster than the bitch does. These interventions are not necessary and may, indeed, be harmful. Unless your veterinarian tells you otherwise, a pregnant bulldog does not need additional food during the first four weeks she is pregnant. If you must give her something extra, make it extra attention.

Begin to increase your bitch's rations gradually during her fifth week of pregnancy. If, for example, she normally eats ¾ cup of dry food and two ounces (56 g) of canned food daily, she could probably use one cup of dry and up to four ounces (112 g) of canned each day by the end of her term. Because living conditions can become crowded in a bitch's abdomen during pregnancy, divide her daily food allotment into three meals when you begin increasing her rations. (In addition to giving their pregnant bitches extra food, some owners switch from regular dry food to puppy chow when a bitch is about six weeks pregnant. Others switch to puppy chow as soon as a bitch has been mated. These changes are permissible unless your veterinarian tells you otherwise.)

Just as overfeeding during pregnancy is counterproductive, so are overdoses of vitamins and minerals. Excess calcium, phosphorous, and vitamin D, for example, can cause bone and kidney damage. Excess vitamin A

There is no one like mom.

can cause coat loss, bone deformities, and liver disease.

Finally, females should not be exposed to teratogens during pregnancy. Defined as substances that disrupt normal embryonic development, teratogens include live-virus vaccines, excess doses of vitamin A, some steroids, and griseofulvin, an antidote for ringworm. These and other teratogenic substances are always potentially harmful to the developing embryo. To be safe rather than sorry, do not give your pregnant female any medications unless they have been prescribed by a veterinarian.

Signs of the Impending C-section

Gestation, the period between conception and birth, lasts between 59 and 67 days after the first successful mating. Puppies are not viable, on average, until day 57 of gestation. About the start of her last week of pregnancy, your bitch may begin to investigate open closets and other locations in search of a nesting place. From then on she ought never to be left alone for more than a few minutes at a time.

Given the choice, most females would spend the last several nights of pregnancy on their owners' beds. In fact, that is where many dogs, pregnant or otherwise, prefer to spend their nights. If anyone objects to this arrangement, the bitch should sleep in her crate in her owner's bedroom. The bedroom door should be kept closed, and children and other pets should be kept at bay. With the bitch close at hand, even comatose sleepers will respond to any unusual noises, ratting about in the crate, or sounds of distress in the night. Do not forget to put water in the crate.

Many breeders begin taking their females' temperatures morning and night with a rectal thermometer on day 58 after the first mating. A dog's normal temperature is between 100° and 102.5°F (37.8° to 39.2°C). If her temperature drops to 99°F (37.2°C) or below, puppies most likely will arrive within 12 hours, although some bitches deliver without exhibiting a drop in temperature, and some deliver more than 12 hours after their temperatures drop. But if the temperature rises two or three degrees above normal, call the vet at once.

Temperature is not the only sign of an impending C-section. Other signs include rapid breathing, pacing, turning around in circles, frequent, somewhat anxious attention to the genital area, and loss of appetite. The more intense these signs become, the closer a bitch is to delivering.

A final sign that birth is nigh is the passing of the placental plug. A gelatinous stopper that forms at the cervix early during gestation to protect the uterus from external infection, the plug is expelled when the cervix begins to relax in anticipation of delivery. The clear, stringy mucus that accompanies the passing of the plug may appear a few hours or a day or two before puppies start to arrive.

As long as a bitch emits a clear, odorless substance, her owner need not worry; but if a dark, green-tinted, odoriferous fluid appears and it is not followed shortly by a puppy, call your veterinarian at once. More than likely a placenta has separated from the wall of the uterus and a puppy is in danger of dying from lack of oxygen— if it has not died already.

Neonatal Puppy Development

When you take your bitch in for her C-section, make sure to take a cardboard box along that is large enough to accommodate her puppies. Put a heating pad in the bottom of the box and cover it with a towel. After you get the puppies home, you can transfer them to their in-house puppy box.

In addition to being lousy at delivering puppies on their own, many bulldog bitches are lousy at motherhood. They have been known to smother puppies by lying on them, to injure or kill puppies by stepping on them, and, in a few cases to harm puppies intentionally. Not surprisingly, most breeders do not recommend leaving

puppies alone with their mothers. The only time puppies should see their mothers is around mealtime, and there should always be someone around to monitor those interactions.

Puppies are ready to begin nursing within one or two hours after being born. When they are not nursing, they should stay in a safehouse, a puppy box made of wood or sturdy cardboard. An adequate sized puppy box measures 32 inches (81.3 cm) by 12 inches (30.5 cm), and is 16 inches (40.6 cm) high. It could have a Plexiglas window in the lid for your viewing convenience, and it should have holes in the side that can be opened for ventilation for your puppies' convenience.

Position a light fixture with a 60-watt bulb in one end of the box to provide heat for your puppies. A light with a rheostat for adjusting heat is the best kind to use. Otherwise, you can adjust the heat by using different bulbs of varying wattage and positioning them at varying distances from the box. The most accurate heat meter is a puppy. If puppies huddle in the end of the box away from the light bulb, the bulb is too strong. If puppies lie directly under the bulb, switch to a bulb of slightly higher intensity. One breeder recommends keeping the box temperature close to 95°F (34°C) the first week, then reducing it to 85°F (28°C) the second week, and to 75°F (22°C) in subsequent weeks.

In addition to proper temperature the puppy box should also have the correct surface. Puppies that lie on a hard, flat surface are apt to become swimmers, i.e., their chests flatten and their legs splay out sideways. As a result they have a hard time getting their legs under themselves. They may also have a hard time breathing because of their flattened chests.

To keep your puppies from developing into swimmers, make sure the floor of their box is soft and nonflat.

A suitable floor can be fashioned out of foam-rubber, egg-crate, hospital-pad material covered with towels. Half-filled hot water bottles or sheets of newspaper wadded into balls—both covered with towels—also make suitable, nonswimming floors.

Feeding Schedule

Puppies need to nurse every two hours for the first week of their lives. This is why few single persons with jobs raise bulldogs. You should prepare a regular feeding station where the mother lies on an old blanket or quilt while the puppies nurse. Be sure to use hydrogen peroxide to clean away any discharge from your bitch's C-section before allowing her puppies to nurse. Prior to their first few feedings, squeeze a few of their mother's nipples to extrude some milk so that the puppies know where meals are being served.

When you squeeze a little milk out of each nipple, check the color of the milk. For the first few days after birth, milk should be white or somewhat yellow. Thereafter it should be a bright, refrigerator white. If your bitch is producing gray or brownish milk or milk with blood in it, she probably has mastitis, an infection of the mammary gland. Call your veterinarian and ask what you should do.

Meanwhile, if only one nipple is producing tainted milk, place tape over that nipple at feeding time to keep the puppies away from it. Continue to monitor milk color each day. If infection is present in more than one mammary gland, the better part of valor consists of hand-feeding the puppies. (See page 84.)

If some puppies are noticeably smaller than the others, allow those puppies to visit the table for several minutes before giving the larger puppies their meal tickets. Watch all the puppies to be sure they are attached

Steady weight gain is an important measure of a puppy's health.

to a nipple and that it is functioning properly. The puppies may nurse for 15 or 20 minutes, and no matter how sleep deprived and cranky you are feeling, allow them to drink all they want before closing the cafeteria. After all, this was your bright idea.

If your bitch does not lick her puppies' nether regions in order to inspire them to urinate and/or to defecate—and if she does not subsequently clean them up, you inherit the job. Dip a cotton ball in warm water and rub the puppies' genital area and anus. Have paper towels on hand for cleaning and drying purposes.

Weigh your puppies each day. They may not gain weight during their first 24 hours. They may even lose a few grams. After that, however, they should gain 7 to 10 percent of their body weight each day for the first two weeks. If a puppy fails to gain weight during any 48-hour period in its first two weeks of life, or if a puppy begins to lose weight, call your veterinarian.

To support this growth, lactating females require prodigious amounts of food, two to three times as much as they would eat normally. It is virtually

impossible to overfeed at this point, so give your girl as much as she wants to eat three or even four times a day. And just to be sure she is getting enough nutrients, feed her puppy chow instead of regular dry food.

Supplemental Feeding

If a puppy is not nursing, if it seems to be crying more than it is nursing, or if it is not gaining weight as it should

If a puppy is not thriving, it must be fed by hand.

be, it most likely will benefit from supplemental feeding. Begin by taking the puppy's temperature with a rectal thermometer that has been lubricated with Vaseline or K-Y Jelly. If the puppy's temperature is below 97°F (36°C), feed it two cc's of dextrose solution that has been warmed to 98°F (36.7°C). When a puppy's temperature falls below 97°F (36°C), enzymes in the puppy's stomach are not functioning well enough to digest milk.

If the puppy's temperature is above 97°F (36°C), feed it two cc's of mother's milk replacer. You can obtain the dextrose solution, the mother's milk replacer, and the syringe with which to administer them from your vet a few days before your bitch is due. Keep the dextrose solution and the milk replacer, once it has been opened, in the refrigerator.

Whether you feed dextrose or milk, the technique is the same. Put a towel on your lap, hold the puppy in one hand, spine side up, at a 45-degree angle to your lap, slide the end of the syringe gently between the puppy's lips, and push the plunger on the syringe a fraction of an inch to release some of the contents of the syringe into the puppy's mouth. Go slowly, pushing intermittently on the plunger as the puppy sucks on the syringe. If the puppy is sucking avidly and then turns its head away, it is probably full. As puppies get a bit older, you can switch to a 4-ounce plastic baby bottle with a nipple.

Puppies too weak to suck dextrose solution or milk from a syringe may have to be tube fed. Ask your veterinarian in advance to show you how to measure the length of tube, attached to a syringe, that needs to be inserted into the puppy's stomach.

Tube feeding, if not done properly, can cause lesions of the pharynx or stomach. If the tube is inserted incorrectly and food is introduced into the lungs, the puppy may choke and die. This method of feeding should be attempted, therefore, only as a last resort.

Weaning Formula

Toward the end of the puppies' third week, you should begin to wean them onto solid food. Begin with a porridge of baby cereal and milk replacer for a few days, then gradually add dry puppy food that has been reduced to powder in a blender. At about four and a half or five weeks, switch to a mixture of canned puppy food and whole dry puppy food that has been soaked in milk. Finally, at about six weeks, switch to canned puppy food or dry food alone.

If hand-raising puppies sounds like work, it is. During several sleep-deprived weeks your determination and self-discipline are all that stand between life and death for the puppies. But you decided to bring them into the world, and you are darn well responsible for seeing them through it.

This tyke looks as if he expects to find coal in his stocking on Christmas morning.

When you have hand-raised a litter successfully, the puppies' progress is a bountiful reward. What's more, the puppies you have nurtured faithfully will be among the best socialized, most people-oriented tykes you will ever see.

Y'all come back, you hear?

The Older Bulldog

Because every bulldog is an individual, his uniqueness will always be part of his makeup and of the aging process as well. Dogs do not all age in the same fashion, nor do they all age at the same rate. A dog's biological age, in distinction to his chronological age, is a function of his genetic background, the quality of his diet, the presence or absence of disease, and the circumstances in which he lives. Because bulldogs are not a long-lived tribe, however, your bulldog can be said to be on the verge of elderly by the time he is six or seven years old.

If you are a first-time owner of an elderly or geriatric dog, you should remember that no one knows your dog as thoroughly as you do. You were the one who carried him outside at one o'clock in the morning for weeks until he finally became house-trained. You found that special chew toy that kept him amused for afternoons on end. You shared your favorite chair and perhaps your pillow with him. Through all those days and years, you came to know the old gent pretty well. Now is the time to use the knowledge you have acquired together to make your dog's life and surroundings as comfortable as possible. To do less would be to neglect an old friend.

The older a bulldog gets, the more comforts he deserves.

Tolls of the Road

The passage of time brings about progressive and irreversible changes in your dog. Sadly, most of the physical changes are not for the better. As your dog's metabolism slows down and his vitality begins to ebb, his senses diminish. He can no longer taste, see, smell, and hear as well as he once did. He is less able to tolerate medication, less able to regulate his body temperature, and less immune to disease. He requires fewer calories to run his body and to maintain his weight. What's more, his thyroid, adrenal, and pituitary glands and his pancreas do not secrete hormones as fluidly as they once did.

These changes are generally accompanied by other physical and behavioral diminutions. His eyes may become cloudy, his muzzle may turn gray, his coat may be less luxuriant, his skin may become more slack, his muscles flabby, and his spine and hips prominent. He may begin to look as though he's wearing a suit that's a few sizes too big for him. He may not hear well, his joints may begin to stiffen, and he may be troubled by varying degrees of lameness. He will most likely become less active, more inclined to sleep, less inclined to accept change, less tolerant of cold temperatures, and, perhaps, a tad irritable.

With the onset of old age a dog becomes more susceptible to disease; therefore, the earlier conditions are diagnosed, the better the chances of recovery. The annual veterinary inspection becomes more important in old age, and you may consider switching to semiannual checkups. Naturally it is important to keep vaccinations current in order to protect against disease.

Old bulldogs are great listeners, and they never correct you for embellishing a story.

Nutrition and the Older Bulldog

As your dog grows older, he may become overweight as a result of his diminished activity and metabolic rate. The signs of excess weight are not difficult to detect. If your dog's abdomen begins to droop, if you cannot feel his rib cage when you run your hands along his sides, if your dog sways more and more noticeably when he walks, or if he develops bulges on either side of the point where his tail joins his body, chances are he is carrying too much weight.

Before putting your bully on a diet, take him to the veterinarian to make sure the excess weight is not being caused by illness. If it is not and if your bulldog is too heavy for his sex and age, switch to lite dog food. Lite food contains 20 to 33 percent fewer calories than regular food does. If you are feeding both wet and dry foods, try a lite dry food for a month. If your dog returns to his "normal" weight, return to regular dry food and continue to monitor his weight. If switching to lite dry does not pare away the padding, continue feeding lite dry and switch to lite canned also.

Like weight gain, progressive weight loss in older dogs is cause for concern—perhaps even more so. Weight loss may indicate kidney failure, the presence of a tumor, diabetes mellitus, liver disease, or other conditions. If your dog loses weight for two consecutive months, schedule an appointment with your veterinarian.

Exercise and Grooming

Although your bulldog may slow down as he gets older, he still needs some exercise. An older dog's participation in play might be limited by arthritis and muscle atrophy, but you can help him to maintain good muscle tone and suppleness, to increase blood circulation, and to improve gastrointestinal motility (the spontaneous movement of the gut) by encouraging him to take part in moderate exercise, the canine equivalent of mall walking done by old-timers. While you and your bully enjoy a walk or a brief playtime, be on the lookout for labored breathing or the rapid onset of fatigue, which may be signs of heart disease.

Frequent grooming—three times a week or so—provides an opportunity to examine your dog for unusual lumps, skin lesions, or external parasites. Lumps or lesions should be examined further by a veterinarian.

A special three-judge panel found the defendant not guilty by reason of immaturity.

Digestive and Dental Concerns

The digestive tract is usually the last system to begin deteriorating in the dog. Some researchers believe that rapid cell turnover in the gastrointestinal tract provides some protection against the degenerative effects of aging. Nevertheless, older dogs are more inclined to constipation than younger dogs are. If this becomes a problem with your older bully, consult your veterinarian before changing your dog's diet or administering a laxative, which can interfere with the absorption of vitamins and minerals.

The time to begin many of the added ministrations that make life more pleasant for older dogs is when they are young dogs. Dental care is perhaps the best example of this advice. Your chances of cleaning your six-year-old dog's teeth, especially if they have never been cleaned before, are not promising. You may need professional help to get the job done at this point, and, by all means, you should seek it. Accumulated tartar can cause gingivitis and weaken tooth structure, making eating a chore at a time when appetite is on the decline for other reasons. Thus, if your dog is young enough at heart to learn new tricks, you should initiate a home dentistry program now (see Pearls Before Teeth, page 48).

The older dogs get, the more conservative they become. They are less adaptable to—and happy about—changes in the environment. Consequently, they should be boarded out only as a last resort when the family goes on vacation. And if they must be boarded, they should be surrounded with familiar toys and other objects from home to cushion the impact of being uprooted. Better still, arrange to have your older dog cared for at home by neighbors, friends, relatives, or a pet sitter.

Moving to a new house or bringing a new pet into your present house are additional sources of stress for an older dog. Moving cannot be avoided sometimes, but you can avoid bringing a new pet home. Indeed, once a dog is entering old age, at roughly the age of six for bulldogs, the chances of a new introduction going smoothly and of a lasting friendship developing between old and young dog are not great.

Saying Good-bye

No matter how well we care for our dogs, they do not last forever. Time will eventually assert its claim on them. When that time comes, we may have to decide between prolonging or ending our dogs' lives. That is a decision in which selfishness has no place. Regardless of how much you want to sustain your relationship with your bully, if your veterinarian tells you that your dog is in pain and the quality of his life is below standard, you owe it to your dog to end that suffering. Remember, the privilege of owning a dog hinges on a crucial bargain: We must add as much to a dog's life as the dog adds to ours. Obviously, to prolong a suffering dog's life simply because you cannot face saying good-bye is to turn that bargain into exploitation.

The sunset years are the time when you should make your dog's life and surroundings as comfortable as possible.

If your veterinarian is willing to come to your house to put your bulldog to sleep, take advantage of that service. Your dog's final moments should be spent in familiar surroundings. If you must take your bully to the veterinarian's office to be put to sleep, do not simply drop him off there. The amount of bad karma such a thoughtless, cowardly act would derive, is too frightening to calculate. Your bully was always there when you needed him—and more than a few times when you did not—you owe it to him to be the last person who holds him when his spirit leaves this body for the next one.

Useful Groups and Addresses

Bulldog Breed Publications

The Bulldogger
4300 Town Road
Salem, WI 53168

Sourmug
No.1 Windy Ridge
Mendota, MN 55150, USA
Telephone: 612-454-9510
Fax: 612-454-9460

Bulldog Club of America
National Officers for 1996–1997

President: Robert Church
3604 Prestwick Drive
Tucker, GA 30084

Vice President: Ana Avarez Sootin
13931 Luray Road
Ft. Lauderdale, FL 33330

Secretary: Toni Stevens
Box 248
Nobleton, FL 34661

Treasurer: James Patterson
3195 Battle Park Way
Marietta, GA 30064

American Kennel Club Delegate
Blanche Deutsch
20-33 Linden Street
Ridgewood, NY 11385

Bulldog Rescue
James and Diane Young
210-340-0055

The Bulldog Mailing List
Send E-mail to "majordomo@io.com"
and place "subscribe *Bulldogx-L* end"
in the body of the message.

Appendix

The bulldog's physical characteristics were developed in order to make him as efficient as possible at hanging onto the muzzle of an enraged bull. When that occupation was no longer fashionable, the bulldog was then bred for success in a different kind of ring: the show ring. The results, some critics believe, were not in the breed's best interests. One writer who praised the 19th century bulldog for its courage, dismissed today's model with the following comment: "Let the reader at once dismiss any notion that these bulldogs [the 19th century kind] were the same monstrosities that we see today, puffing and panting after any minor exertion."

Monstrosity, like beauty, is in the eye of the beholder, and it is not our place here to make up anyone's eyes or mind. We simply reproduce below the bulldog standard according to the American Kennel Club, and let the reader make up his or her own mind. Whether you see the bulldog as beauty or beast, you will at least know what the people who breed them think they ought to look like. That opinion, of course, constitutes neither an aesthetic nor a moral imperative.

The Bulldog Standard

The perfect Bulldog must be of medium size and smooth coat; with heavy, thickset, low-swung body, massive short-faced head, wide shoulders and sturdy limbs. The general appearance and attitude should suggest great stability, vigor and strength. The disposition should be equitable and kind, resolute and courageous (not vicious or aggressive), and demeanor should be pacific and dignified. These attributes should be countenanced by the expression and behavior.

Size

The size for mature dogs is about 50 pounds; for mature bitches about 40 pounds.

Proportion

The circumference of the skull in front of the ears should measure at least the height of the dog at the shoulders.

Symmetry

The "points" should be well distributed and bear good relation one to the other, no feature being in such prominence from either excess or lack of quality that the animal appears deformed or ill-proportioned.

Influence of Sex

In comparison of specimens of different sex, due allowance should be made in favor of the bitches, which do not bear the characteristics of the breed to the same degree of perfection and grandeur as do the dogs.

Head

Eyes and eyelids. The eyes, seen from the front, should be situated low down in the skull, as far from the ears as possible, and their corners should be in a straight line at right angles with the stop. They should be quite in front of the head, as wide apart as possible, provided their outer corners are within the outline of the cheeks when viewed from the front. They should be quite round in form, of moderate size,

In addition to its usefulness for transporting food, a picnic hamper makes a swell resting place.

the ears, should measure at least the height of the dog at the shoulders. Viewed from the front, it should appear very high from the corner of the lower jaw to the apex of the skull, and also very broad and square. Viewed at the side, the head should appear very high, and very short from the point of the nose to occiput. The forehead should be flat (not rounded or domed), neither too prominent nor overhanging the face.

Cheeks. The cheeks should be well-rounded, protruding sideways and outward beyond the eyes.

Stop. The temples or frontal bones should be very well defined, broad, square and high, causing a hollow or grove between the eyes. This indentation, or stop, should be both broad and deep and extend up the middle of the forehead, dividing the head vertically, being traceable to the top of the skull.

Face and muzzle. The face, measured from the front of the cheekbone to the tip of the nose, should be extremely short, the muzzle being very short, broad, turned upward and very deep from the corner of the eye to the corner of the mouth.

Nose. The nose should be large, broad and black, its tip set back deeply between the eyes. The distance from bottom of stop, between the eyes, to the tip of the nose should be as short as possible and not exceed the length from the tip of nose to the edge of underlip. The nostrils should be wide, large and black, with a well-defined line between them. Any nose other than black is objectionable and a brown or liver-colored nose shall disqualify.

Lips. The chops or "flews" should be thick, broad, pendant and very deep, completely overhanging the lower jaw at each side. They join the underlip in front and almost or quite cover the teeth, which should be

neither sunken nor bulging and in color should be very dark. The lids should cover the white of the eyeball, when the dog is looking directly forward, and the lid should show no haw.

Ears. The ears should be set high in the head, the front inner edge of each ear joining the outline of the skull at the top back corner of skull, so as to place them as wide apart, and as high, and as far from the eyes as possible. In size they should be small and thin. The shape termed "rose-ear" is the most desirable. The rose ear folds inward at its back lower edge, the upper front edge curving over, outward and backward, showing part of the inside of the burr. (The ears should not be carried erect or prick-eared or buttoned and should never be cropped).

Skull. The skull should be very large, and in circumference, in front of scarcely noticeable when the mouth is closed.

Jaws. The jaws should be massive, very broad, square and "undershot," the lower jaw projecting considerably in front of the upper jaw and turning up.

Teeth. The teeth should be large and strong, with the canine teeth or tusks wide apart, and the six small teeth in front, between the canines, in an even, level row.

Neck, Topline, Body

Neck. The neck should be short, very thick, deep and strong and well arched at the back.

Topline. There should be a slight fall in the back, close behind the shoulders (its lowest part), whence the spine should rise to the loins (the top of which should be higher than the top of the shoulders), thence curving again more suddenly to the tail, forming an arch (a very distinctive feature of the breed), termed "roach back" or, more correctly, "wheel back."

Body. The brisket and body should be very capacious, with full sides, well rounded ribs and very deep from the shoulders down to its lowest part, where it joins the chest. It should be well-let-down between the shoulders and forelegs, giving the dog a broad, low, short legged appearance.

Chest

The chest should be very broad, deep and full.

Underline

The body should be well-ribbed-up behind with the belly tucked up and not rotund.

Back and Loin

The back should be short and strong, very broad at the shoulders and comparatively narrow at the loins.

Tail

The tail may be either straight or "screwed" (but never curved or curly), and in any case must be short, hung low, with decided downward carriage, thick root and fine tip. If straight, the tail should be cylindrical and of uniform taper. If "screwed," the bends or kinks should be well-defined, and they may be abrupt and even knotty, but no portion of the member should be elevated above the base or root.

Forequarters

Shoulders. Should be muscular, very heavy, widespread and slanting outward, giving stability and great power.

Forelegs

The forelegs should be short, very stout, straight and muscular, set wide apart, with well-developed calves, presenting a bowed outline, but the bones of the legs should not be curved or bandy, nor the feet brought too close together.

Elbows

The elbows should be low and stand well out and loose from the body.

Feet

The feet should be moderate in size, compact and firmly set. Toes compact, well-split-up, with high knuckles and very short stubby nails. The front feet may be straight or slightly out-turned.

Hindquarters

Legs. Hind legs should be strong and muscular and longer than forelegs, so as to elevate loins above shoulders. Hocks should be slightly bent and well-let-down, so as to give length and strength from loins to hock. Lower leg should be short, straight and strong, with stifles turned slightly outward and away from the body. Hocks are thereby made to approach each other, and the hind feet to turn outward.

Feet. Should be moderate in size, compact and firmly set. Toes compact, well-split-up, with high knuckles and short stubby nails. Hind feet should be pointed well-outward.

Coat and Skin

Coat. Should be straight, short, flat, close, of fine texture, smooth and glossy. (No fringe, feather or curl.)

Skin. The skin should be soft and loose, especially at the head, neck and shoulders.

Wrinkles and dewlap

The head and face should be covered with heavy wrinkles, and at the throat, from jaw to chest, there should be two loose pendulous folds, forming the dewlap.

Color of Coat

The color of coat should be uniform, pure of its kind and brilliant. The various colors found in the breed are to be preferred in the following order: 1.) red brindle; 2.) all other brindles; 3.) solid white; 4.) solid red, fawn or fallow; 5.) piebald; 6.) inferior qualities of all the foregoing.

Note: A perfect piebald is preferable to a muddy brindle or defective solid color. Solid black is very undesirable, but not so objectionable if occurring to a moderate degree in piebald patches. The brindles to be perfect should have a fine, even and equal distribution of the composite colors. In brindles and solid colors a small white patch on the chest is not considered detrimental. In piebalds the color patches should be well-defined, of pure color and symmetrically distributed.

Gait

The style and carriage are peculiar, his gait being a loose-jointed, shuffling, sidewise motion, giving the characteristic "roll." The action must, however, be unrestrained, free and vigorous.

Temperament

The disposition should be equable and kind, resolute and courageous (not vicious or aggressive), and demeanor should be pacific and dignified. These attributes should be countenanced by the expression and behavior.

Index